CREDIT CARD AND DEBT MANAGEMENT:

A STEP-BY-STEP HOW-TO GUIDE FOR ORGANIZING DEBTS AND SAVING MONEY ON INTEREST PAYMENTS

SCOTT BILKER

PRESS ONE PUBLISHING, Barnegat, New Jersey

CREDIT CARD AND DEBT MANAGEMENT:
A STEP-BY-STEP HOW-TO GUIDE FOR ORGANIZING DEBTS AND SAVING MONEY ON INTEREST PAYMENTS

By SCOTT BILKER

Published by:

PRESS ONE PUBLISHING
PO Box 563, Barnegat, NJ 08005-0563
Tel: (609) 660-0682 **Fax:** (609) 660-1412
E-mail: PressOne@cybercomm.net
URL: http://www.DebtSmart.com

Copyright © 1996 by Scott Bilker
First Printing 1996
20 19 18
Printed in the United States of America

Library of Congress Catalog Card Number: 95-71626

Publisher's Cataloging in Publication
   (Prepared by Quality Books Inc.)

Bilker, Scott.
   Credit card and debt management : a step-by-step how-to guide
for organizing debts and saving money on interest payments / Scott
Bilker.
   p. cm.
   Includes index.
   ISBN 0-9648401-9-7

   1. Finance, Personal. 2. Consumer credit. 3. Credit cards.
I. Title.

HG3756.U6B55 1996   332.024
                          QBI95-20540

For my wife Larissa and our children; Brandon, Grant and Brooke.

TABLE OF CONTENTS

INTRODUCTION...8

CHAPTER 1: IMPORTANCE OF MANAGEMENT 11

CHAPTER 2: DEFINING THE PROBLEM 14

    TYPES OF CREDIT 14
    GETTING CREDIT 15
    WARNING SIGNS 16
    QUESTIONS THAT NEED ANSWERS 17
    DEBT MANAGEMENT 18

CHAPTER 3: GETTING ORGANIZED 19

    TOOLS OF THE TRADE 19
    FILES 20
    BILLS-UNPAID FILE 21
    CREDIT CARD GRAVEYARD 21
    CREDIT OFFERS 21
    SORTING MAIL 21

CHAPTER 4: LISTING CREDIT CARDS AND TERMS 22

    MAXIMUM LENDING TIME 23
    WORKSHEET USAGE SUMMARY 23

CHAPTER 5: MATH AND MONEY...31

    WHAT CONSTITUTES A LOAN..32
    RELATIONSHIPS BETWEEN LOAN VARIABLES 35
    TIME-REMAINING TABLES 36
    CALCULATING THE MONTHLY PAYMENT....................................39
    CALCULATING THE TIME REMAINING ON THE LOAN 41
    CALCULATING THE APR 42
    CALCULATING THE PRINCIPAL...43
    CALCULATING THE UNPAID BALANCE 43
    MORE REAL-LIFE EXAMPLES..46
    PROBLEMS 48
    SOLUTIONS 50

CHAPTER 6: MODEL SOLUTIONS..54

    LEARN BY EXAMPLE...54
    NEED FOR A MODEL..54
    APPROACHING THE PROBLEM 56
    ELEMENTS OF THE MODEL...56
    DOLLAR-WEIGHTED AVERAGE INTEREST RATE 58

CHAPTER 7: LOAN CALCULATION WORKSHEET 61

    SIMPLER REPRESENTATION...61
    WORKSHEET USAGE SUMMARY 61
    EXAMPLE WORKSHEET 62
    BLANK LOAN CALCULATION WORKSHEET..................................64

CHAPTER 8: **PAYMENT SCHEDULE WORKSHEET** **65**

    INCOME 65
    OTHER MONTHLY PAYMENTS 66
    EXAMPLE PAYMENT SCHEDULE..68
    WORKSHEET USAGE SUMMARY 69
    BLANK PAYMENT SCHEDULE 71

CHAPTER 9: **CREDIT SOLUTIONS** **72**

    GOALS 72
    LOWERING YOUR INTEREST RATES 73
    PAYING A LITTLE MORE 73
    CALCULATING SAVINGS...75
    FINDING LOWER RATES...78
    ACCURACY OF MODEL 79
    LOWEST POSSIBLE MONTHLY PAYMENTS..............................81
    HOW MUCH MORE DEBT CAN YOU TAKE 81

CHAPTER 10: **CHOOSING THE BEST CREDIT CARD: FEES AND EFFECTS** **83**

    FEES 83
    WHAT TO COMPARE...86
    FUTURE VALUE COMPARISON 88
    INCENTIVES 94

CHAPTER 11: **PAYING THE BILLS** **96**

    SORTING THE BILLS-UNPAID FILE 97
    BALANCING YOUR CHECKING ACCOUNT 98
    BLANK CHECKING ACCOUNT BALANCING WORKSHEET 100
    CREATE NEW WORKSHEETS..102

CHAPTER 12: **CREDIT USAGE TIPS AND HABITS** **103**

CHAPTER 13: **BAD ADVICE** **109**

APPENDIX

    1: **TIME-REMAINING TABLES** **116**

    2: **BALANCE & PAYMENT FACTORS** **132**

    3: **TRUE APR FOR SECOND MORTGAGES**...................**135**

INDEX...**138**

ACKNOWLEDGMENTS

Writing this book was truly one of the most challenging experiences of my life. It would not have been possible without the help of some very talented individuals. I want to thank my wife, Larissa, for her technical editing and support. My parents, Harvey L. and Audrey L. Bilker, (accomplished authors with three books and hundreds of short stories and articles published to date) for their suggestions and editing. Claude Tygier of Berier Financial Services and creator of the Burmese Tiger Technical System, for his expert advice, insight and editing which took this work to a new level. Robert B. Gamble for his support, review of the mathematical details and editing. Paul S. Bilker for his copyright and trademark guidance. Barry W. Wainwright for his help with the title. Richard and Barbara Crammer for their support, editorial and graphic design suggestions. Dave Hoffman for his editing, cover design recommendations, and creative writing guidance. Frank and Jen Baglino and Joe and Jen Macedo for their encouragement and continuing support.

WARNING - DISCLAIMER

Everyone's financial situation is different. This book is designed to provide information in regard to the subject matter covered. It is sold with the understanding that the publisher and author are not engaged in rendering legal, accounting, financial planning, or other professional services. If legal or other expert assistance is required, the services of a competent professional should be sought.

It is not the purpose of this manual to reprint all the information that is otherwise available to the author and/or publisher, but to complement, amplify and supplement other texts. You are urged to read all the available material, learn as much as possible about credit cards/debt management, and to tailor the information to your individual needs. For more information on this subject visit your library or ask a trusted financial professional where you can locate more details pertaining to your personal finances.

Credit card and debt management alone will not entirely solve all your credit problems, it is a methodology for organizing and understanding some aspects of your overall financial situation. For many people, this organization and understanding is enough to make them more aware of their spending and therefore, aid in relieving credit burdens by saving money on interest payments.

Every effort has been made to make this book as complete and as accurate as possible. However, there **may be mistakes;** typographical, mathematical or in content. Therefore, this text should be used only as a general guide and not as the ultimate source of credit card and debt management information. Furthermore, this book contains information on this subject only up to the printing date.

The purpose of this book is to educate and entertain. The author and Press One Publishing shall have neither liability nor responsibility to any person or entity with respect to any loss or damage caused, or alleged to be caused, directly or indirectly by the information contained in this book.

The information, methods and techniques described by the author are based on his own experience. They may not work for you and no recommendation is made to follow the same course of action. No representation is made that following the advice in this book will work in your case. The author and publisher expressly disclaim any and all warranties, including but not limited to warranty of fitness for particular use.

INTRODUCTION

In my early twenties, I realized I needed to begin establishing a positive credit history. Having little knowledge of loans and credit, I decided to search the library for books on this subject. I read an informative book about obtaining credit and followed the author's advice.

The initial strategy was simple. First, I applied for department store and gasoline credit cards because they are the easiest to acquire. After making a few purchases with these cards and paying them on time, I had the credit history needed to begin applying for major credit cards.

In less than a year, I had a total of four major credit cards and six store and gasoline cards. I only used my credit lines for necessities, such as college-related expenses and tuition, living expenses, emergency car repairs and food.

Having very few cards, it was easy to manage the bills. I needed a checking account and a simple list containing each card name, the balance and due date — there wasn't much paperwork. I kept the credit card statements in the original envelopes and filed them in a cardboard magazine folder — in no particular order. The balances were small and effortlessly paid from month to month.

It wasn't long before new credit cards arrived and charges built up, then my student loans came due. The paperwork began to pile up and I was spending too much time managing these various accounts. Not only was there a problem with organizing the different accounts but paying on time became increasingly difficult since due dates were scattered throughout the month.

These factors combined with the day-to-day cost of living forced me to create a system for organizing my debts. Luckily, I had a strong background in mathematics and was not intimidated by the necessary calculations or planning involved.

The first step in creating a plan was identifying the details of these problems and what I needed to gain from the solutions.

Some of those considerations were:

1. **SAVE TIME WHEN ANALYZING MY DEBT.** There were so many different monthly payments that I was spending a considerable amount of time trying to figure out my next move. I wanted to get the most productive work done in the shortest amount of time so I would not be burdened with money problems on a daily basis.

2. **MAKE ACCURATE PREDICTIONS.** Each payment was due at a different time during the month. *Timing is everything and mine was off.* I needed to save enough money each week in order to pay bills when the statements arrived.

3. **ORGANIZE THE PAPERWORK.** My box of statements had grown so large I could not find anything. When I needed to reference checks and charges, it took too much time and effort to locate specific information.

4. **ORGANIZE THE DEBT.** Having many credit cards and loans translates to many balances at different rates. I did not know how much debt I had or how long it would take to pay it off. Without that information, I could not plan for future purchases or determine if I was in trouble from overcharging.

5. **SAVE MONEY.** Worst of all I spent so much money paying interest that my original balances were never being reduced. I had to find a way to compare different loans and credit cards to reduce the interest payments.

I was not alone. After speaking with friends and family, I found my situation was not unique. In each case the problems were similar and everyone I spoke with had a way to deal with them — ranging from complete denial of the situation to extremely detailed. I wanted to learn from other people before I spent time developing my own method of organizing debt. Unfortunately, I did not find all the answers I was looking for. I could not find the comprehensive guide I was in search of. Most books had too many worksheets with details I did not need. They talked about investing, net worth, and accounting. Investment strategies will hopefully be just as important to me sometime in the future but at this point I needed to gain more control of my credit. I had to read numerous books on mathematics of finance, credit, loans, mortgages and money management before I had all the facts I needed.

I developed my own worksheets that solved problems relating **specifically** to credit cards and loans. These *worksheet tools* were vital to my understanding of *where I stood* with each loan. I learned that being disciplined and following through are the most important habits in managing debt.

After almost ten years of using and refining a systematic approach to credit management, I have saved *thousands* of dollars in interest payments and handled involved debt situations effectively. I know *where I stand* all the time and never wonder whether I will be able to pay the bills on time or if I can afford to use my credit cards. The most rewarding benefit is that I have never been late with any payments, and I only have to devote three hours every two weeks to money matters.

These techniques have been very successful for me and others with whom I have shared them. Friends and acquaintances are continuously seeking my advice on matters of credit. I am confident that with this guide you too will find solutions to your financial situation while learning to be more effective at debt management.

CHAPTER 1

IMPORTANCE OF MANAGEMENT

Credit cards as we know them today are relatively new and continuously evolving. The major laws protecting consumers' rights involving credit were passed in the mid-seventies. In the early eighties, even with high interest rates, the credit industry started to explode. By the mid-eighties, the volume of credit cards issued was staggering. Banks that wanted a piece of the market began offering incentives to entice consumers into switching to them. Although the market for credit was growing, most people were using the cards as a convenience rather than as loans. Many people paid their entire balance each month. Banks do not make money this way since a grace period for purchases, where no interest is charged for one month, is usually standard. As far as banks are concerned, the best customer for credit is one who pays the minimum each month and on time.

According to The Nilson Report, credit card debt hit $273.4 billion in 1992 and is expected to rise to $436.8 billion by the year 2000! **Credit card debt is rising quickly and banks are competing heavily for your business.** It is now more important than ever to be effective at managing debt. This is especially true for people living from paycheck-to-paycheck who must dip into their credit sources to make ends meet. **Our country is quickly becoming a nation of debtors with the average credit card holder in possession of almost ten cards!** The people who learn how to plan their credit spending and repayment are rewarded with extended lines of credit and better rates. Those who are not efficient and disciplined with their credit have very few options available once banks learn their credit history.

Not only can debt be a financial problem, it can also be a source of emotional pain. The number-one subject of arguments, and divorce, for married couples is money. What to buy? What to cut back on? What to borrow? Pulling yourself out of the red may very well solve many family conflicts.

Today, obtaining credit is a necessity. An inexpensive, reliable new car costs nearly $12,000. Although most people would like to pay in cash, the reality is they need a loan. The rates and terms of that loan will be determined by your credit history which is easily obtainable from numerous credit bureaus throughout the country who specialize in keeping an up-to-date record of all credit users. If you have used credit wisely in the past and repaid previous loans on time, you will be in a favorable position. If not, the result will be a more costly loan with higher interest rates.

Not only do banks use your credit history to determine your credit worthiness but employers, landlords and businesses read this report to access your track record of financial responsibility. Credit cards are not a luxury! They are required financial tools. If you travel you need your credit card to book flight reservations and reserve hotel rooms. You also need a credit card to rent cars and buy products by telephone. Being without a credit card today would make your life as difficult as traveling by horse and buggy. Credit cards are a business standard!

This book is intended to assist you in creating a *road map* for your unique financial situation. Each chapter will guide you step-by-step through various aspects of analyzing your debt with the use of specialized worksheets. By following realistic examples you will learn how to summarize your financial position, making it more manageable.

The process of going through each of these exercises is of great importance if you wish to take control of your money and manage your debt more effectively. Like an athlete preparing for a competition, you will need to practice certain techniques. You may find parts of this book to be technical and detailed; however, this should not be feared. Money, interest, payments, and cost analysis are subjects that must be explored thoroughly if you want to receive the maximum benefit. You need to make good financial decisions and save the most money possible.

If you are not prepared with the facts regarding your personal spending and debt, you could receive a bad credit deal. You must understand the fine print when borrowing. Knowing, in advance, how much the principal, interest, and payments are is crucial. **You must be able to figure out how much you can afford to borrow based on your current monthly bills and spending before entering a loan which might be too demanding on your income.**

The methods described in the following chapters have proved exceptionally useful in managing large amounts of debt. These systems of analyzing debt are the starting point in making decisions for your future. Can I afford that new car? How can we save money for a house and pay back our creditors? How much money do I need to pay the debt back within a reasonable time?

The use of computers is the most effective and accurate way to track your spending and calculate information about specific loans. However, I want this book to be a stand-alone reference guide to solving debt problems. The tables and worksheets included in this book eliminate the need for financial calculators and computers for the examples that will be discussed.

Even when supplied with all the knowledge and information available, it will serve no purpose unless you take action — **discipline is the key.** Taking time to investigate your debt and credit will make the difference between losing control of your money and taking control. Learning everything you can about credit cards and loans is the only way to find solutions to saving money and paying off your debts.

CHAPTER 2

DEFINING THE PROBLEM

TYPES OF CREDIT

There are four types of credit transactions, each with its own set of requirements. Even if you are familiar with credit cards and loans, it is worth understanding the basics of each type since the chances are high that you will, someday, encounter all of them in your financial life.

1. **Unsecured, open-end** — Unsecured means there is no physical property backing the loan which the lender could take back if the loan is not repaid. Credit cards are an example of this type of credit, which is revolving (open-end). Revolving credit is when you can use the line of credit granted by the bank as soon as you repay it. If you owed $1,000 and paid back $300 you would be able to use that $300 to make new purchases. As the principal decreases, the unused amount of the credit line increases enabling the borrower to use it again. With unsecured, open-end credit the borrower receives a specific limit which is backed by credit worthiness. The borrower must maintain a minimum payment against the principal and interest.

2. **Secured, closed-end** — An example of this is a mortgage or car loan. The borrower secures the loan with collateral (physical property) which can be repossessed by the lender if the borrower defaults on the payment. This loan carries a specific payment and lasts a specific amount of time. The loan is closed-end because of the limitation in amount and time where the only way to obtain new credit is receiving a new loan.

3. **Unsecured, closed-end** — This is sometimes called a signature loan. Payments and times are specific and determined when the loan is taken. This is also based on the borrowers credit worthiness but is <u>not</u> revolving.

4. **Secured, open-end, or open-end equity** — This loan is based on the equity (amount of value in a property above the amount still owed) in the collateral, which is usually a house. This type may be revolving with payment terms similar to that of credit cards.

GETTING CREDIT

Most of this book is directed towards handling existing debt, but if you need to establish or re-establish your credit, use these five tips to get started.

1. **Get a checking *and* savings account.** You must furnish this information on any credit application and it looks better to have both accounts. Banks that loan you money want to know that you can write them a check every month.

2. **Apply for gasoline and department store credit cards.** These are the easiest to obtain. The interest rates are high, but there is usually no annual fee. Make a few purchases and pay on time. <u>Do not max out your cards!</u> This will get you in trouble before even owning major credit cards. The goal after acquiring these cards is building a credit history. This *credit resume* you develop should reflect a good payment record.

3. **After a few months of using the store and gas credit cards, begin applying for major credit cards.** If you created a positive credit history there will be no problem obtaining MasterCards and Visa Cards. If you find banks are refusing to grant you credit lines, you will want to apply for a secured card.

4. **A secured major credit card will be easier to get.** A secured credit card is a line of credit backed by your personal savings (or other) account. Go to a local bank and open an account. Deposit $500 to $1000 and ask for an application for a secured card. The bank will most likely extend credit in the amount of your deposit. You will not have access to your money but you will have a major credit card with a charging limit equal to the amount you deposited in your account. Use the secured card for purchases and pay on time. Then you can begin applying for unsecured credit cards.

5. **If you still need to build your credit history after owning a secured credit card, cash advance the maximum limit on that card, take the money to another bank, and follow the same procedure to get another secured credit card.** You can do this many times and receive numerous lines of credit, but you will be making payments on all of them right away. It will be costly, but you will establish your credit history.

For example, you deposit $1,000 at BankOne in a new savings account and apply for a secured credit card. BankOne grants you a secured credit card with a $1,000 maximum limit. You advance $1,000 from your credit line at BankOne, take the money to BankTwo, and deposit it in a new savings account. Now you have a $1,000 balance on the BankOne Card with a minimum monthly payment of $35. You then apply for a secured credit card from BankTwo, they agree to extend this credit since your card is secured by the savings account. You are given another card with a $1,000 limit from BankTwo. The result is two major credit cards; BankOne with a $1,000 balance and $35 monthly payments, and the other card from BankTwo with $1,000 of open credit (available to use). Also, you have two savings accounts with $1,000 (which you cannot touch). Now credit bureaus are reporting that you are responsibly handling two major credit cards — this is your ultimate goal.

WARNING SIGNS

If your debt seems overwhelming, don't feel guilty or helpless. What is important now is finding a way out, a way to make good on your promise to repay the debt. Today there are so many opportunities for obtaining credit. Banks are fighting to get good customers. If your credit record is clean, you will receive the best offers available.

Even if you feel that your credit is under control, problems can still creep up on you. The following ten warning signs are a starting point to determine how troubling your credit problems may be. If any apply to you, it is time to work a little harder at understanding credit.

1. You don't have enough money in the bank to pay bills when they are due.
2. You do not know the exact dollar value of your debt.
3. You have so many bills that you are writing checks every day.
4. Your checks are bouncing.
5. You are getting turned down for new credit.

6. You are arguing with your spouse about spending and debt.
7. You are unsure if you can afford to buy new items.
8. You are continuously worried about your debt.
9. Creditors are threatening to turn over your account to a collection agency.
10. Collection agencies are calling.

QUESTIONS THAT NEED ANSWERS

The problem is too much debt and not enough money. The ultimate solution is more income, but this may not always be possible. To effectively manage your debt there are some basic questions you should <u>always</u> be able to answer.

1. How much is my total short term debt? This would include credit cards, auto loans, and personal lines of credit.
2. How much money do I pay towards this debt per month?
3. How long will it be before all my debt is paid off?
4. What is my total line of credit; cash and charges?
5. What is the rate of interest on all the debt I have?
6. How much money can I afford to spend given my debt situation?
7. What options do I have that could help me reduce my debt?
8. How much money do I need to save weekly to pay my bills on time?
9. Is my credit history good?
10. What is my minimum monthly payment?
11. How much is my net income?

This book and the worksheets contained herein are designed to answer these questions and provide a new understanding of your debt. The answers to these questions are the foundation of your financial life. You cannot make informed decisions for spending if you do not know this information. It takes some time to find the answers but it also saves time in the future.

While many people spend a considerable amount of time planning different aspects of their lives, very few spend enough time reviewing their spending and finances. Your financial position is constantly changing, and you would not want to deal in a desultory manner with as important a matter as money management. You cannot be sloppy in your thinking or bookkeeping. You must be neat and organized with both.

DEBT MANAGEMENT

1. **KNOWLEDGE.** It is well known that *knowledge is power*. Believe it. You must have an understanding of your credit predicament if you want to change it. You must run your personal finances like any good business owner manages company funds. Surely, most people have some idea of how money is flowing through their accounts, but the ability to use this information wisely is a different matter.

2. **SIMPLIFICATION.** Because your situation is unique and complex, it is necessary to simplify the work involved. You must understand how the handling of one loan affects another. How picking one credit card over others changes the cost of borrowing. This is done by "modeling" the details of each case and drawing conclusions based on certain calculations.

3. **TIMING.** The most important criterion for good credit is **paying on time**! The only way to accomplish this is to have the money in the bank *before* the payment is due. You do not want checks to your creditors to bounce.

4. **PLANNING.** *If you fail to plan, you plan to fail!* Another truism. Always plan carefully. If you were going on a long vacation, you would pack all important items. Likewise, debt management requires planning and attention to detail.

5. **HAPPINESS.** If you are continuously worrying about making the next payment you will not be very happy. If you are arguing with your spouse over which loan is better or what to buy, there will be increased stress in your relationship. The simple solution is to become more knowledgeable about money and credit.

Many people despise paying interest on debt. They believe it is just an overpriced way for banks to rip off the public. The interest paid during the course of a loan is the price to "buy" the use of that money today. Most consumers have no problem paying fees for other items or services and at the same time feel that interest on debt is robbery. **Lenders do deserve compensation for allowing customers to use their money. However, some deals are better than others and it is just a matter of becoming knowledgeable about which cards are available and which are the best deals.** By examining your debt and calculating your position, you will find solutions which yield a better deal on interest and payments.

CHAPTER 3

GETTING ORGANIZED

TOOLS OF THE TRADE

Organization is the key to credit card and debt management. The first step to organization is finding a place in your home to serve as your office. This area must be equipped with a table, chair, and room for files. Once you establish your bill-paying office you must furnish it with the right tools.

Every profession has its own set of tools, and the ones you will need for handling your finances are available in the stationary section of any store. It is important that all necessary items for paying bills and managing money are present when you begin planning your financial strategy.

Here is a shopping list of items needed to become more organized:

☐ Calculator
☐ Checking account
☐ Checkbook with Transaction
 Register
☐ Daily planner
☐ Envelopes
☐ Filing cabinet (two drawer, 18
 inches deep)
☐ Hanging files
☐ Paper
☐ Paper clips

☐ Pens and pencils
☐ Personal address book
☐ Scissors
☐ Scotch tape
☐ Postage Stamps
☐ Stapler & Staples
☐ Staple remover
☐ Table or desk
☐ Telephone book

Take time now to review this list and check off what you have. I consider these items essential for basic office work. If any items are missing from this inventory, I recommend procuring them as soon as possible.

FILES

Your files will prove to be the most valuable asset in organization. Files store all your vital information and clear the house of paper clutter. Once everything is in the proper file, you will be able to reference information quickly. Most people prefer hanging-files over the standard manila type. Hanging-files use metal supports, so each file can move freely in the cabinet.

After you are finished assembling the hanging-folders in your filing cabinet, set up these specific file headings:

- ☐ Auto Insurance
- ☐ Bills Unpaid
- ☐ Cable TV
- ☐ Credit Cards - one file for each, by bank name and type.
     For example: CitiBank MasterCard.
- ☐ Credit Offers
- ☐ Electric
- ☐ Financial Records
- ☐ Gas/Oil
- ☐ Important Documents - birth certificates, Social Security Cards, diplomas, titles, marriage certificates, etc..
- ☐ Loans - by bank and type (car, second mortgage, etc..).
     For example: CoreStates Student Loan.
- ☐ Medical Expenses
- ☐ Phone
- ☐ Rent or Mortgage
- ☐ Receipts
- ☐ Subscriptions
- ☐ Taxes
- ☐ Water/Sewer

Once the files have been created and alphabetized, begin filling them with the appropriate papers. Gather and file all the paperwork from around the house, some of which may be stuffed away in a cabinet or shoe box. Knowing all of your paperwork is sorted, labeled and easily retrieved should also bring you a great deal of satisfaction.

Once you create your organized office, keep it clutter-free at all times. Do not allow paper or other items to pile up on the desk. This area should always be ready for you to sit down and take care of business.

BILLS-UNPAID FILE

This is the most important file in the cabinet and will be used on a daily basis. It stores all bills to be paid and other paperwork that needs attention.

This file holds everything that needs your immediate action, including non-bill-related items. Keeping the important paperwork in this file guarantees that no items are missed when you pay bills.

CREDIT CARD GRAVEYARD

This file contains all plastic cards that are not currently in use, accounts you have but will not be needing at the moment. You only need to carry one credit card with you; the rest are stored here until you decide to use them.

CREDIT OFFERS

You are undoubtedly bombarded by banks soliciting your business. Use the Credit Offers file to store these pre-approved notices and applications for bank loans. Instead of throwing these advertisements away, save offers that seem like a possibility for future credit. You will be looking in this file for options to reduce your current interest rates.

SORTING MAIL

Going through the daily mail can be a time-consuming and arduous task, but one that must be done _every_ day. Sort through and dispose of the junk mail and open each bill. Take out the fluff (direct mail advertisements) that does not interest you, staple the billing statement to the return envelope and file it in the Bills-Unpaid File.

CHAPTER 4

LISTING CREDIT CARDS AND TERMS

Now that you organized the paperwork, it is time to begin organizing your credit cards. Most people have a plethora of credit cards and/or loans. These open lines of credit are needed for *buying* new money (borrowing). All cards are not equal; some have better policies than others depending on your particular situation. The only way to know about each line of credit is to examine the Account Agreement that came with the card. Always file your agreements so they are available for reference.

Instead of keeping all Account Agreements in a pile and looking through them each time you're comparing different bank policies, or retrieving them from their individual files, it is more efficient to list the information on the **Credit Card InfoSheet** (see pages 26 and 29). This comprehensive listing includes all pertinent information required to analyze and compare different credit cards. This worksheet is another valuable tool you will refer to often. By listing account information on this sheet, you save considerable time by only referencing this one sheet for the most important bank policies.

To better organize pending loans you will use the **Credit Offer InfoSheet** (see pages 27 and 30). These are the cards or credit lines that you might not need right away but could consider in the future. All the information for credit offers is conveniently located in the Credit Offer File you set up after reading the previous chapter. Both worksheets' column headings are identical and contain the same information. You will refer to the Credit Offer InfoSheet when cards you already own are not offering the best deal. If the banks that currently hold your credit card accounts cannot produce the most cost-effective borrowing, you want to search for better deals.

The worksheets are broken into three sections:
1. General
2. Cash
3. Charge

There can be a difference in how the banks handle charges and cash advances. Sometimes interest rates are higher for cash advances, or the cash advance maximum limit is different from the purchases limit.

MAXIMUM LENDING TIME

The only new piece of information calculated on these worksheets is the Maximum Lending Time. Each credit card has an interest rate and a Minimum Payment Policy. With this information and the Time-Remaining Tables, located in the Appendix, it is easy to find the Maximum Lending Time each credit card allows you to borrow money.

This number is used for comparing lending times and Minimum Payments. The true Maximum Lending Time for most credit cards is between 12 to 25 years. This is because the Minimum Payment decrease as the unpaid balance (principal) in the account decreases. The Maximum Lending Time you compute represents the length of time it takes to pay off the initial amount of the loan at the current interest rate, if today's Minimum Payments are made for the entire length of time. This means that the Maximum Lending Time value is valid as long as payments are kept the same.

Comparing Maximum Lending Times is a way to quickly determine which bank, with today's terms, lends money for a longer amount of time. Generally, the longer the time, the lower the monthly payment. Lower monthly payments are a very important option when money is getting tight.

WORKSHEET USAGE SUMMARY

1. **Credit Card** - the name of the bank and type of card (Master, Visa, etc.).

General

2. **Account Number** - make sure every digit is accurate so you can use this sheet when calling your bank with questions.

3. **Phone Number** - most banks have an 800 number which should be used since you are not charged for the call.

4. **Annual Fee** - very important in considering which card to use. Many cards do not carry this fee.

   Minimum Payment Policy - this policy is used to compute the monthly payment. Some banks calculate the Minimum Payment by multiplying the balance by a percentage; for example, 2%. If the balance is $2,000 then the Minimum Payment is ($2,000 x .02) = $40. Other banks use a divisor of the balance; for example; *divide the balance by 50. In this case, if the balance is $5,000 then the Minimum Payment is:* $\frac{\$5,000}{50} = \$100$.

   Most banks also have an absolute Minimum Payment which is used if the calculated payment was less than a specific amount. A sample Minimum Payment Policy is: **2% of the balance or $20, whichever is greater.**

   I will use a shorthand notation for this policy: **2% > $20**. The symbol > means **greater than,** and the notation is read as: 2% (of balance) greater than $20.

   The notation is a compact way to represent the policy so the important numbers are more visible while using the worksheet.

6. **Latest Offers** - this includes the newest and best deals the bank is offering. This may be lower rates for a certain period of time, cash back bonuses, etc..

Cash

   Advance Fee Policy - this fee is charged for withdrawing money from a cash machine or writing a check against your credit line. An example policy would be: **2% of the amount advanced but not less than $2 or greater than $20.**

   If you are borrowing $2,000 cash from a card with this policy, the fee would be $20 because 2% of $2,000 is $40 and $40 is greater than the maximum fee of $20. I will represent this cash advance policy with the following notation: **$2 < 2% < $20**.

8. **Interest Rate** - this is the interest rate for *cash advances only*.

9. **Limit** - the maximum amount of *cash* you can borrow.

10. **Maximum Lending Time** - this is the maximum time for cash advances and is determined by using the Time-Remaining Tables in the Appendix. You need the Minimum Payment Policy and the interest rate to find this number. If the Minimum

Payment Policy is calculated by a divisor (dividing the principal by a number), then the process is simple. Find the closest interest rate column in the table, look down the column and find the closest number to the divisor. The time is listed on the far left rows in years and months.

For example, *the divisor is 33 for the Minimum Payment Policy and the interest rate is 17.9%. Looking at the Time-Remaining Tables in the 18% column, the closest number to 33 is 33.0565. Therefore, the Maximum Lending Time is 3 years 10 months. Abbreviated 3-10 (3 years-10 months).*

When the Minimum Payment Policy is a percentage of the balance, the percentage must first be inverted (divided into one). For example, *the Minimum Payment Policy is 2.5% of the balance and the interest rate is 8%. First, find the number you need to look up by dividing .025 into 1 or $\frac{1}{.025} = 40$. Looking at the Time-Remaining Tables in the 8% column the closest number to 40 is 40.2350. Therefore, the Maximum Lending Time would be 3 years 11 months. Abbreviated 3-11.*

The next chapter is devoted to using the Time-Remaining Tables to solve credit problems. Example 5.5 clearly illustrates the use of the tables to find the time when you know these numbers.

Charges

11. **Interest Rate** - only for charges.

12. **Limit** - maximum dollar amount of charges allowed.

13. **Maximum Lending Time** - the procedure to find this is the same as discussed in the Cash section. The only difference is that you use the charge interest rate to find the value.

Note: If the interest rate and limit terms are the same for cash and charges only fill out the cash section of the worksheet.

EXAMPLE WORKSHEETS

CREDIT CARD INFOSHEET

Credit Card	GENERAL					CASH				CHARGES		
	Account Number	Phone	Annual Fee	Minimum Payment Policy	Latest Offers	Advance Fee Policy	Interest Rate	Limit	Maximum Lending Time	Interest Rate	Limit	Maximum Lending Time
Credit Card 1	123487968765 4340	(800) 123 4567	None	1/33> $20	No fee balance transfers until October 5.	$2<2%< $20	18.9%	$2,500	3-11			
Credit Card 2	653958730695 8360	(800) 657 2345	None	1/33> $20	No fee balance transfers until August 8.	$2<2%< $20	8.9%	$4,000	3-2			
Credit Card 3	475869709485 3420	(800) 384 9685	None	1/33> $20	No fee balance transfers until July 17.	$2<2%< $20	11.75%	$4,000	3-2			
Store Card 1	76523456	(800) 485 9785	None	2.5%> $15	15% discount (one time offer)					19.8%	$1,000	5-7
Store Card 2	54986756	(800) 243 9347	None	1/25< $20	None					21%	$800	5-7

CREDIT OFFER INFOSHEET

	GENERAL					CASH				CHARGES		
Credit Card	Account Number	Phone	Annual Fee	Minimum Payment Policy	Latest Offers	Advance Fee Policy	Interest Rate	Limit	Maximum Lending Time	Interest Rate	Limit	Maximum Lending Time
Future Card 1	N/A	(800) 740 8253	None	1/40<$10	Pre-approved through June 15.	None	14.9%	$5,000	4-8			
Future Card 2	N/A	(800) 547 9761	$50	1/33<$20	Pre-approved through August 5.	None	11.9%	$5,000	3-0			
Future Card 3	N/A	(800) 489 4587	$15	1/33<$20	Pre-approved through July 10.	$2<2%<$20	19.8	$3,500	4-0			
Future Card 4	N/A	(800) 124 5679	$50	2.5%<$20	Pre-approved through September 26.	$2<2.5%	17.9%	$3,500	5-2			
Future Store 1		(800) 243 9347	None	1/25<$20	Pre-approved through September 20.					21%	$800	5-7

WORKING WITH THE WORKSHEETS

Always use a pencil when filling in the worksheets since the information will change quickly. Review the example cards listed in the worksheets. Notice the format and notation used in each block. As a practice exercise, check the numbers for the Maximum Lending Time using the procedures discussed.

Make photocopies of the blank worksheets and fill out the information for your lines of credit. If you have a question about any bank policies, call that bank. Representatives are usually available 24 hours a day, 7 days a week.

The Credit Card InfoSheet is also a valuable reference if your credit cards are ever lost or stolen. The phone numbers and account information allow you to quickly contact each bank and inform them about the situation.

BLANK WORKSHEETS

CREDIT CARD INFOSHEET

Credit Card	GENERAL					CASH					CHARGES		
	Account Number	Phone	Annual Fee	Minimum Payment Policy	Latest Offers	Advance Fee Policy	Interest Rate	Limit	Maximum Lending Time	Interest Rate	Limit	Maximum Lending Time	

CREDIT OFFER INFOSHEET

| Credit Card | GENERAL | | | | | | CASH | | | | | CHARGES | | |
	Account Number	Phone	Annual Fee	Minimum Payment Policy	Latest Offers	Advance Fee Policy	Interest Rate	Limit	Maximum Lending Time		Interest Rate	Limit	Maximum Lending Time

CHAPTER 5

MATH AND MONEY

I want to begin this chapter with a personal story. My father asked me to help him pick out a new car. After visiting several new car dealers in the area we finally found one with a car that had the price and features we were looking for.   Once the negotiations were complete, and the price was agreed upon, it was time for the dealership to add in those extras such as; tags, processing fees and anything else they could.

Finally, the balance due for the car was presented and we decided to finance it. The salesman told me the length of the loan and the interest rate. I already knew the amount to be financed so it was easy to calculate the monthly payments. It was at this time that we were instructed to go into a separate office to read and sign the loan agreement.

When the contract came out of the computer the monthly payment shown was $65 a month higher than I had calculated! That $65 per month for entire length of the 5-year loan would total $3,900! I expressed my concern and was told that, "you can't figure out monthly payments with a simple calculator" and "the computer is right." I informed the salesman that unless the payments were what I computed, the deal was off and I would be visiting the dealer across the street who would be happy to have my business. Furthermore, I was using a scientific calculator which can easily handle simple monthly payment problems.

Once they saw I was serious, it was explained that the computer "accidentally" added a charge on for an extended warranty and undercoating. They adjusted for this error that they "obviously had no idea occurred", and told me the new payment. This time it was closer, but still off by $10 a month. This might not seem like much money but $10 a month for 60 months is $600 and I would rather keep the $600 than contribute it to the next dealership rob-the-customer-day party. I told them again that they were wrong and I was not going allow my father to sign any agreement until the numbers were correct!

After searching, they finally "discovered" what went wrong. Another computer blip that they had no control over. It turned out that the interest rate on the agreement was not the one they originally quoted me. Once all the numbers were correct the computer spit out the correct monthly payment and we got the car.

I am not trying to imply the dealership tried to rip me off. Oh, no! But what is certainly true is that if I did not know how much the payment was supposed to be, my father might have signed that agreement and paid a huge unnecessary fee.

Since then I have helped many of my friends buy cars. In each case, the starting monthly payment was always higher than I calculated and later reduced to the correct number. These are real examples of the necessity of being able to solve simple math problems.

This is the most important chapter in the book. It is essential to know how to calculate, in advance, all the terms of a loan. You need this information to compare different credit agreements and determine which is best for your unique situation.

The math is easy. You only need to know the basics: addition, subtraction, multiplication and division. All other complex calculations are provided by tables in the appendix.

This chapter also includes many exercise problems. It is suggested that you do all the problems so you have a full understanding of the material. There are several example problems that serve as a guide. All the exercise problems are relevant and closely represent the way things are in the real world. **These are not exercises to drill theoretical math into your head but are intended to provide the minimum amount of background needed to grasp the important concepts.**

When you are finished with this chapter, you will be ready to analyze the details of almost any loan. When you are negotiating a loan with a car dealer, you will know, in advance, what the payment terms should be.

WHAT CONSTITUTES A LOAN

There are only four variables involved in a loan: principal, interest, time and payments. That's all. The dollar cost of the interest and many other aspects of a loan can be determined from this basic information. If you know how to figure each out you will never be confused with this subject again.

PRINCIPAL

The principal is the initial amount of money that is being borrowed. This amount might include all fees associated with the loan. The principal is also equal to any outstanding balance. For example, if you charged something for $5,000 today, then the principal is $5,000. If you made payments toward that principal for one year and the outstanding balance shown on your statement is $3,500, you could say the <u>new</u> principal is $3,500.

The principal is the amount of money that is considered the starting point for calculating the interest, payments, or length of the loan. Credit cards charge interest on the *average daily balance*. This average daily balance is calculated by adding up the balance (principal) of the account for every day in the billing cycle (one month) then dividing by the number of days in that cycle. This result is the average daily balance and considered the principal for that billing cycle. Most credit cards use the average daily balance to calculate the monthly finance charges. I consider this to be the fairest way to charge interest on a revolving line of credit.

INTEREST RATE

There are many types of interest rates, but the most important, when it comes to understanding loans, is Annual Percentage Rate. APR (Annual Percentage Rate) is the interest rate when all information about the loan is taken into consideration. All credit cards quote an APR but this is not the <u>true</u> APR because they do not include fees when computing that rate. **We will always try to identify the true interest rate so we can compare one loan to another in our effort to save money.**

The APR quoted for credit cards and some loans should be 12 times the monthly rate of interest. Therefore, if the monthly interest is 1% then the APR is 12% which is 12 times 1%. This monthly percentage is multiplied by the unpaid balance (principal) to compute the periodic finance charges. The number of periods is 12, one for each month of the year.

Example 5.1:

What is the amount of interest charged, in one month, on a loan with an outstanding balance (principal) of $1,000 if the APR is 24%?

Solution 5.1:

If the APR is 24% then the monthly rate is 24% divided by 12 which is 2% per month. The interest charged is 2% of the outstanding balance or .02 multiplied by $1,000.

Interest Charge = .02 x $1,000 = $20

You can also calculate the APR being charged from the monthly interest.

Example 5.2:
A loan with an outstanding balance of $2,000 is showing an interest charge of $32 for the month. What is the APR for the loan?

Solution 5.2:
First, you must find the percentage of interest charged on the loan. This is $32 divided by $2,000 or $\frac{\$32}{\$2,000} = 0.016$. To convert 0.016 to a percentage you multiply it by 100; i.e., 0.016 = 1.6%. This is the monthly (periodic) rate of interest; therefore, the APR is 12 times this rate.

APR = 12 x 1.6% = 19.2%

It's very important to be able to determine whether the amount of interest being charged is correct. Granted, most of the time the bank is correct, but I have had experiences where the numbers on my statement did not add up.

TIME

Time is the term that is used to describe the length of the loan. This is how long it will take to pay off a loan that starts today, with a specific APR and a certain payment schedule. The time it takes to pay off a loan is of great concern. You want to know how much of your future earnings will be tied up in a credit agreement. Also, you need to ask yourself if the item which you are purchasing is worth committing money to for that long.

The time of the loan is indicated in years but the important number is periodic payments. Periodic payments are the number of payments made when interest is charged. In the case of most loans and all credit cards I know of, interest is charged monthly. Therefore, there are 12 periods in the year or one period for each month. If a loan is paid off in 3 years it could also be said to be paid off in 36 payments or 36 months.

PAYMENTS

When payments are indicated in a loan they are meant to be paid periodically. The period is usually monthly. The payment is a central consideration in deciding which credit card or loan to accept. You may want lower payments because your monthly budget is tight; however, you might want to save money on total interest charges by paying the loan off faster with higher payments.

RELATIONSHIPS BETWEEN LOAN VARIABLES

All four of the loan variables (principal, interest, time and payments) are dependent on each other. This means that by changing the value of one these, you will change the value of another. They are connected mathematically, and by adjusting each of them, you change many key elements of your loan. By understanding how they are related, you will be able to answer questions like:

1. If I have $150 a month to spend on a loan at 13% how much can I borrow?
2. What is the payment for a $3,000 loan at 12% for 5 years?
3. What is the true interest rate (APR) on a 3-year loan for $2,000 if I'm paying $62.67 a month?
4. What do I owe on a 5-year auto loan for $10,000 at 9% that I've been making payments on for 18 months?
5. How long does it take to pay back a $6,000 debt at 8% if the payments are $99.61 a month?

These are remarkably consequential questions that must be addressed if you want to manage your debt effectively. How could you go shopping for something as expensive as a car and not figure out *in advance* how much you are able to finance? How can you continue using your credit lines without knowing how it will affect your future income? How can you know which credit card to use when transferring balances?

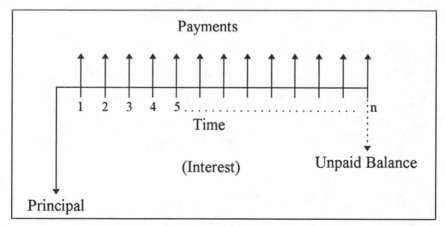

Figure 5.1: Cash Flow Diagram.

Figure 5.1 shows the relationship of all the components of a typical loan. The arrows pointing down are the amount of money that is borrowed or owed, while the arrows pointing up are the amount paid at some particular periodic time. Money is borrowed at time zero — the day you get it. The numbers on the time line indicate the period; in most cases this will be months. The small "n" means some time in the future —

this varies depending on the terms of the loan. Interest is present everywhere during the loan and is computed by the bank after every payment. Finally, the Unpaid Balance is the amount owed (it is pointing down) at some time "n" in the future. If a loan is paid off completely at time "n" then the Unpaid Balance is zero and the arrow is not shown.

Notice that the payments must come <u>after</u> the money is borrowed. I know this is obvious, but try to understand that by looking at the Cash Flow Diagram. The diagram shows the flow of money with the arrows. When you receive money the arrows point down, when you spend money the arrows point up. This way you can quickly identify which direction the money is flowing and when the transactions are occurring. Whenever you set up any loan problem it is important to identify the value of the loan components and where, in time, they are in relation to each other.

I am involved with a tutoring program at a local high school. Students ask me repeatedly, "What is math good for? I'm never going to use algebra after high school!" Being an engineer, I appreciate math for its theoretical value and disciplined logic. Science changes as new discoveries are made and old theories must be altered or replaced to explain what is observed. In mathematics there will never come a day when someone says, "two plus two equals five." **But the most important use of math that is common to everyone is money!** The math involved in loans and borrowing is not complicated but I doubt the majority of people can answer all the questions listed in the beginning of this section. Even though I attended an engineering college, these questions were not introduced until I had a class in engineering economics. I realized that up until that point I did not have a good understanding of this subject.

TIME-REMAINING TABLES

The Time-Remaining Tables in the appendix are provided to simplify the math needed to solve problems related to loans. These tables identify the relationship between the principal, interest, time and payments through the use of the Principal-to-Payment Ratio which we will refer to as the RATIO. The RATIO is simply the principal divided by the payment.

Example 5.3:
What is the RATIO for a loan if the principal is $5,000 and the payment is $100?

Solution 5.3:
Divide the payment into the principal to find the RATIO.

$$RATIO = \frac{\$5,000}{\$100} = 50$$

$$RATIO = 50$$

The RATIO represents the relationship of the principal and the payment. These RATIOs make up the body of the table and are shown in columns for various interest rates and rows of various times. This representation indicates that there is a certain time *related* to a particular RATIO and interest rate. Figure 5.2 is part of one Time-Remaining Table.

Time Remaining on Loans

18% to 21.5%
3 to 6 years

Years	Months	18.00%	18.50%	19.00%	19.50%	20.00%	20.50%	21.00%	21.50%
3	1	28.2371	28.0375	27.8399	27.6442	27.4506	27.2588	27.0690	26.8812
3	2	28.8051	28.5966	28.3903	28.1862	27.9842	27.7842	27.5863	27.3904
3	3	29.3646	29.1473	28.9322	28.7195	28.5090	28.3007	28.0946	27.8907
3	4	29.9158	29.6895	29.4657	29.2443	29.0252	28.8086	28.5942	28.3822
3	5	30.4590	30.2236	29.9908	29.7607	29.5330	29.3079	29.0852	28.8650
3	6	30.9941	30.7495	30.5078	30.2688	30.0325	29.7988	29.5678	29.3394
3	7	31.5212	31.2675	31.0167	30.7688	30.5238	30.2815	30.0421	29.8053

Figure 5.2: Time-Remaining Table Example.

In large type, 18% to 21.5%, indicates the range of rates included in this table. Also, 3 to 6 years shows the times that are listed in the table. All of the tables provide these headings so you can quickly locate the table that applies to the problem you're solving.

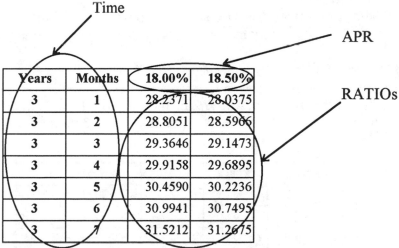

Figure 5.3: Time-Remaining Table Example.

Figure 5.3 describes the "anatomy" of the table by circling critical areas. The first step in using the tables is being able to look up specific numbers. Follow the next few examples to learn how the table is used.

Example 5.4:
What is the RATIO for a loan with an APR of 18% and a payoff time of 3 years 5 months (41 payments = 3 x 12 + 5)?

Solution 5.4:
Find the column for 18% and follow it down to the row that shows 3 years 5 months. The number in that block is the RATIO.

$$RATIO(18\%, 3\text{-}5) = 30.4590$$

The notation, RATIO(18%,3-5), means "the RATIO for 18% at 3 years 5 months" is equal to 30.4590.

Years	Months	18.00%	18.50%
3	1	28.2371	28.0375
3	2	28.8051	28.5966
3	3	29.3646	29.1473
3	4	29.9158	29.6895
3	5	30.4590	30.2236
3	6	30.9941	30.7495

Figure 5.4: Solution for example 5.4.

Example 5.5:
What is the Time Remaining on a 18.5% loan with a RATIO of 29?

Solution 5.5:
Find the column for 18.5% and follow it down to the closest number to 29. Follow that row to the left and find the Time Remaining.

$$Time(18.5\%, 29) = 3\text{-}3$$

The notation, Time(18.5%,29), means "the Time Remaining for a 18% loan with a RATIO of 29" is equal to 3 years 3 months (39 payments).

Years	Months	18.00%	18.50%
3	1	28.2371	28.0375
3	2	28.8051	28.5966
3	3	29.3646	29.1473
3	4	29.9158	29.6895
3	5	30.4590	30.2236
3	6	30.9941	30.7495

Figure 5.5: Solution for example 5.5.

Example 5.6:
Find the APR for a loan with a RATIO of 30.25 and a Time Remaining of 41 payments.

Solution 5.6:
Payments made for 41 months are made for 3 years and 5 months. Find the row for 3 years and 5 months and follow that row to the closest number to 30.25. Follow that column up and locate the APR.

$$APR(3\text{-}5, 30.25) = 18.5\%$$

The notation, APR(3-5,30.25), means "the APR for a 3-year, 5-month loan with a RATIO of 30.25" is equal to 18.5%.

Years	Months	18.00%	18.50%
3	1	28.2371	28.0375
3	2	28.8051	28.5966
3	3	29.3646	29.1473
3	4	29.9158	29.6895
3	5	30.4590	30.2236
3	6	30.9941	30.7495

Figure 5.6: Solution for example 5.6.

Examples 5.4, 5.5, and 5.6 show all three uses of the Time-Remaining Tables. If you can look up the number and follow these examples, you are ready to begin solving some interesting loan problems.

CALCULATING THE MONTHLY PAYMENT

Now that you are familiar with the Time-Remaining Tables, the process of finding the Monthly Payment is simple. Since there is a relationship between the RATIO and the payment you must use the tables to find the payment.

Remember, there are four variables to every loan: principal, interest, time and payments. If you know three of these variables you can always figure out the fourth. Therefore, to compute the monthly payment of any loan you <u>must</u> know:

1. Principal
2. Interest
3. Time

Any problem that does not indicate these three components of the loan does not have a defined monthly payment. The question is ambiguous unless those parameters are included in the problem.

The steps to finding the Monthly Payment for any loan are:
1. Make sure you know the principal, APR and time.
2. Find the RATIO associated with APR and time as in example 5.4.
3. Divide the RATIO into the principal and the result is the Monthly Payment.

Example 5.7:
What is the Monthly Payment that will pay off a $2,400 loan in 2 years at 12% APR?

Solution 5.7:
Step 1:   Principal = $2,400   APR = 12%   Time = 2 years

Step 2:   Find RATIO(12%,2-0) = 21.2434 using tables (see page 120).

Step 3:   Divide $2,400 by 21.2434

$$\text{Monthly Payment} = \frac{\$2,400}{21.2434} = \$112.98$$

Monthly Payment = $112.98

If the time and/or the APR do not exactly match what is in the table, use the closest numbers. In that case your answer will not be exact but it will be a very close approximation. For example, if example 5.7 asked for an APR of 11.9%, you still must use 12% since this is the closest to 11.9%. Therefore, the solution is exactly the same, but the true Monthly Payment for a 11.9%, $2,400, 2-year loan is $112.86. The difference is only 12¢.

The types of questions you can to solve from this section are:
1. What is the monthly payment on a loan?
2. Which monthly payment is cheaper when given many loans to review?
3. How does the length of the loan affect the monthly payment?

CALCULATING THE TIME REMAINING ON THE LOAN

This will be extremely important later for finding out how long you will be in debt. When you know the payoff time for your debt it is easier to plan payments and purchases.

Just as in the previous section, you need three of the four loan variables to find the Time Remaining on a loan.

1. Principal
2. Interest
3. Payments

The steps to finding the Time Remaining to pay off any loan are:

1. Make sure you know the principal, interest, and payment.
2. Find the RATIO by dividing the principal by the payment as in example 5.3.
3. Use the RATIO and interest to locate the Time Remaining as in example 5.5.

Example 5.8:

What is the Time Remaining on a $5,000 loan at 9% APR with payments of $100 per month?

Solution 5.8:

Step 1:   Principal = $5,000   APR = 9%   Payment = $100

Step 2:   Calculate the RATIO.

$$\text{RATIO} = \frac{\$5,000}{\$100} = 50$$

Step 3:   Use the RATIO and APR to find the Time Remaining (see page 118).

Time(9%,50) = 5-3 (5 years 3 months)

The types of questions you can solve from this section are:

1. How long will it be before any particular loan is paid off?
2. How long will it be before all my debt is paid off?
3. Is the payoff time on the loan correct?
4. How do different credit card policies affect payoff times?
5. What is the maximum length of time a credit card will lend money?

CALCULATING THE APR

Sometimes you receive offers for products that allow you to make payments for a certain period of time. You also know the total cost of the product. With this information you can calculate the interest that is being charged and compare that to other credit cards you own to determine whether to take the payment plan or use your credit for the purchase.

The information needed to find the APR is:
1. Principal
2. Payments
3. Time

The steps to finding the APR on any loan are:
1. Make sure you know the principal, payments and time.
2. Find the RATIO by dividing the principal by the payment as in example 5.3.
3. Use the RATIO and time to find the APR as in example 5.6.

Example 5.9:

What is the APR on a $8,500 loan with payments of $174.39 per month for 5 years?

Solution 5.9:

Step 1:   Principal = $8,500   Time = 5 years   Payment = $174.39

Step 2:   Calculate the RATIO.

$$\text{RATIO} = \frac{\$8,500}{\$174.39} = 48.7413$$

Step 3:   Use the RATIO and Time to find the APR (see page 118).

$$APR(5\text{-}0, 48.7413) = 8.5\%$$

The types of questions you can solve from this section are:
1. Based on the APR, which credit card or payment plan is better?
2. What is the true APR after I include all the fees for borrowing?
3. How do payment, time and principal affect the APR for the loan I'm considering?

CALCULATING THE PRINCIPAL

The information needed to find the principal is:

1. Payments
2. Interest
3. Time

The steps to finding the principal of any loan are:

1. Make sure you know the payment, interest and time.
2. Find the RATIO using the interest and time as in example 5.4.
3. Multiply the RATIO by the payment. The result is the principal.

Example 5.10:

What is the Principal of a loan with payments of $120 for 3 years and an APR of 12%?

Solution 5.10:

Step 1:   Payment = $120   Time = 3 years   APR = 12%

Step 2:   Find RATIO(12%,3-0) = 30.1075 (see page 120).

Step 3:   Multiply the RATIO and the payment.

Principal = 30.1075 x $120 = $3,612.90

The types of questions you can solve from this section are:

1. How much money can I borrow based on the loan terms and what can I afford monthly?
2. How do I find the original amount of a loan if I know all the payment, time and rate information?
3. How can I compare the different starting balances for various credit cards and loans?

CALCULATING THE UNPAID BALANCE

The previous sections demonstrated techniques for finding the fundamental variables of a loan given the proper information. The section deals with an application of those basic concepts which surfaces often when determining how your payments affect your future debt. The focus is on applying your knowledge of the tables and loan variables to find the *future* principal of a loan. It is true that the unpaid balance of a loan can also be called the principal however, for the purpose of understanding this section, unpaid balance may mean the principal of the loan at some time in the future and principal may mean the balance of a loan at some time in the past.

For example, if you *have* a loan of $10,000 (principal) at 10% and *will be* making $250 monthly payments, you may be interested in knowing what you *will owe* (unpaid balance) after 12 payments, 24 payments, etc. This example refers to the principal in the present and unpaid balance in the future.

This same example can be stated as follows: You *had* a $10,000 (principal) loan at 10% and have made 12 monthly payments of $250 and want to know what your unpaid balance is *today*. This way of presenting the example refers to the principal in the past and the unpaid balance in the present. Both examples are asking the same question. You start with a principal, interest, and payment; make those payments for a certain amount of time and want to know what is still owed.

When you are referring to an unpaid balance in the future, it can be called the *future* principal or the future value. Future value will be discussed in greater detail in the following chapters. It is important to be able to calculate future unpaid balances so you know what your debt will be in the future and have a plan for handling it. This way you are able to have a continuous strategy both current and for the future.

The information needed to find the unpaid balance is:
1. Payments
2. Interest
3. Time
4. *Original* Principal

The steps to finding the future unpaid balance of any loan are:
1. Make sure you know the payment, interest, time, and *original* principal of the loan.
2. Find the RATIO using the interest and time as in example 5.4.
3. From the original principal, subtract the RATIO multiplied by the payment.
4. From 12, subtract the RATIO multiplied by the interest rate.
5. Divide the result in step 3 by the result in step 4.
6. Multiply the result in step 5 by 12.

Steps 3 through 6 can be expressed by the formula:

$$\text{Unpaid Balance} = 12 \times \left[\frac{\text{Original Principal } - \text{ (RATIO} \times \text{Payment)}}{12 - \text{(RATIO} \times \text{Interest)}} \right]$$

Example 5.11:
You have made 20 monthly payments (1 year, 8 months) of $300 on a $13,000 loan at 14% APR. What is your unpaid balance?

Solution 5.11:
Step 1:   Principal= $13,000   Payment = $300
                    Time = 1 years, 8 months   APR = 14%

Step 2:   Find RATIO(14%,1-8) = 17.7463 (see page 123).

Step 3: $13,000 - (17.7463 X $300) = $7,676.11

Step 4:   12 - (17.7463 X 0.14) = 9.5155

Step 5: $7,676.11 ÷ 9.5155 = $806.70

Step 6:   12 X $806.70 = $9,680.40

Unpaid Balance = $9,680.40

Using the formula:

$$\text{Unpaid Balance} = 12 \times \left[\frac{\$13,000 - (17.7463 \times \$300)}{12 - (17.463 \times 10.14)} \right]$$

$$= 12 \times \left[\frac{\$7,676.11}{9.5155} \right]$$

Unpaid Balance = 12 X $806.70 = $9,680.40

Type of questions you can solve from this section are:
1.   What will I owe on a loan in the future based on the payments I make today?
2.   Which loan will I owe less on in the future based on the terms of each loan and my method of payment?

MORE REAL-LIFE EXAMPLES

These examples use the same concepts learned in this chapter but may be a little trickier.

HOW MUCH DO I OWE?

Example 5.12:

I have a 5-year auto loan for $10,000 at 9% APR. The payments are $207.58 per month. I want to pay an extra $50 per month to reduce the principal more quickly. The extra $50 plus the original payment bring the total to $257.58 per month. In 18 months I think I will be able to pay off the entire loan in one payment. How much will I owe at that time?

Solution 5.12:

The first thing you should ask is: *What loan variable is the question asking for — principal, interest, payments or time?* Example 5.12 is asking for the outstanding balance which is also the principal. This principal however is in the future, therefore, you need to follow example 5.11 for the solution and find the unpaid balance. The original principal is $10,000, the question is; what *will the* principal of the loan be in 18 months?

The only part of this problem that may be confusing is the payment. The loan was written to have a $207.58 monthly payment but you are paying an extra $50 per month. It is important to remember that what you really pay is the only consideration. The real payment being made here is $257.58 ($207.58 + $50) which is used to find the future unpaid balance.

Follow example 5.11

Step 1: Principal = $10,000, Payment = $257.58, Time = 1 year, 6 months, APR = 9%

Step 2: Find RATIO(9%,1-6) = 16.7792

Step 3: $10,000 - (16.7792 X $257.58) = $5,678.01

Step 4: 12 - (16.7792 X 0.09) = 10.4899

Step 5: $5,678.01 ÷ 10.4899 = $541.28

Step 6: 12 X $541.28 = $6,495.36

Unpaid Balance = $6,495.36

Summary of solution.

    1. Realize you are looking for the unpaid balance.

    2. Find the true payment being made.

    3. Follow the example that most closely resembles the problem.

PAYMENT PLAN OR CREDIT CARD?

Example 5.13:

A product that you want to buy costs $240. The company has a payment plan available which allows you to make 12 equal payments of $20 plus a $2.00 monthly fee. You also have a choice of using a 12% APR credit card. Should you use the company payment plan or charge $240 on the card?

Solution 5.12

Step 1:

How do you make a comparison that indicates which plan is better? You can pay any amount towards a credit card but you must make specific payments with the company's plan. The easiest way to compare these two options is by checking the respective interest rates. Even though the company is not directly stating that they are charging interest the fact is the $2.00 monthly fee can be considered interest. Since the company fee does not change it makes it difficult to immediately see how much interest is being charged.

Step 2:

If we simply restate the question it is clear how to go about making the comparison. *What is the APR on a $240 loan with payments of $22 per month ($20 + $2.00) for 12 months (1 year)?* This is similar to example 5.9.

$$\text{RATIO} = \frac{\$240}{\$22} = 10.9091$$

$$APR(1\text{-}0, 10.9091) = 18\%$$

Since the company plan is charging a rate of 18% and your credit card is only 12% it makes more sense to charge it! The trick here is to restate the question so it matched one of the example problems. **All loan related questions can be restated like one of the examples.**

SUMMARY

Millions of people use credit and most are unaware of how these transactions are affecting their future. The methods discussed in this chapter are the foundation of the math needed to find the solutions when comparing different loans and payment options. Once you have mastered these basic concepts you will be prepared to deal with many financial situations.

Do all the exercises at the end of the chapter. **There are no trick questions!** Every problem is straightforward and can be solved by reviewing the examples and following their solutions. The answers and step-by-step solutions to all exercise problems are shown following the exercises.

Keep in mind that all possible interest rates and times are not included in the Time-Remaining Tables, therefore you may have to choose the closest number to find an answer.

When trying to solve the problems it is important to first identify what piece of loan information you are attempting to find. You will be looking for principal, interest, payments, or time.

PROBLEMS

1) What is the monthly interest charged on a credit card with an outstanding balance of $2,500 if the APR is 19.8%?

2) What is the RATIO for a loan with a principal of $6,500 and monthly payments of $365?

3) If you have $8,000 of debt at 9% APR, what monthly payment must be made to pay it off in exactly 4 years?

4) You noticed an interest charge of $21.80 on the monthly statement of your loan that has an outstanding balance (before finance charges) of $2,400. The loan interest rate shown on the statement for that period is 8.9% APR. Is the interest charge correct?

5) You need to know the original principal for a car loan. You've lost the sales contract and have been making payments of $252.02. You remember that the interest rate was 9.5% and the loan is for 5 years. What is the original loan amount?

6) Your credit card claims to have a grace period on charges. This means they do not charge you any interest if you pay the balance off in full each month. But they do have a minimum finance charge of $0.50. If you buy one item on your card that cost $12, what is the APR created by the minimum finance charge?

7) You can only afford $150 a month to finance a new car loan. The loan would be for 5 years at 13% APR. How much can you borrow?

8) What is the monthly payment that pays off a $1,000 loan in 1 year 6 months at 19.8% APR?

9) What is the time remaining on a 14% APR loan with a RATIO of 38.2744?

10) How long does it take to pay off a $3,000 loan at 8.9% APR if you are paying $59.19 per month?

11) Find the APR for a loan with a RATIO of 44.0594 and a Time Remaining of 4 years, 5 months.

12) What is the APR of a $15,600 loan with payments of $281 per month for 7 years?

13) What was the cost of the interest in the loan from example 5.12?

14) You have been paying $683.93 monthly toward your 30 year mortgage of $88,000 for 8 years. What is the unpaid balance?

SOLUTIONS

1) Follow example 5.1. If the APR is 19.8% then the monthly rate is 19.8% divided by 12.

$$\text{Monthly Rate} = \frac{19.8\%}{12} = 1.65\% = .0165$$

Interest Charge = .0165 x $2,500 = $41.25

----

2) Follow example 5.3. The RATIO is the principal divided by the payment.

$$\text{RATIO} = \frac{\$6,500}{\$365} = 17.8082$$

----

3) Follow example 5.7. Find RATIO(9%,4-0) = 40.1848. The monthly payment is the principal divided by the RATIO.

$$\text{Monthly Payment} = \frac{\$8,000}{40.1848} = \$199.08$$

----

4) Follow example 5.2. The interest charge is *not correct*. The monthly interest is equal to the interest charge divided by the balance.

$$\text{Monthly Interest Rate} = \frac{\$21.80}{\$2,400} = .009083 = .9083\%$$

APR = 12 x .9083% = 10.9% which is not the promised 8.9%.

This can also be solved by comparing the amount of the interest charged rather than the APR. Following example 5.1, if the APR is 8.9% then the monthly rate is 0.7417%.

Interest Charge = .0074167 x $2,400 = $17.80

Since the bank charged $21.80 instead of $17.80 the interest charge is not correct.

----

5) Follow example 5.10. Find RATIO(9.5%,5-0) = 47.6148. The original principal is the payment multiplied by the RATIO.

Principal = 47.6148 x $252.02 = $12,000

----

6) Follow example 5.2. The monthly interest is equal to the interest charge divided by the balance. In this case the interest is the $0.50 fee.

$$\text{Monthly Interest Rate} = \frac{\$0.50}{\$12} = 0.04167 = 4.167\%$$

APR = 12 x 4.167% = 50%

Notice how high that APR is for a card that claims to have a grace period! This is another example of why you must **do the math!**

----

7) Follow example 5.10.

RATIO(13%, 5-0) = 43.9501

Principal = 43.9501 x $150 = $6,592.52

----

8) Follow example 5.7. Since there are no columns with exactly 19.8% use the closest which is 20%.

RATIO(20%, 1-6) = 15.4409

$$\text{Monthly Payment} = \frac{\$1,000}{15.4409} = \$64.76$$

This is only an estimate because the tables do not contain the exact interest rate needed for the RATIO. The actual monthly payment is $64.67. Obviously the estimate is close enough for real life problems given that the difference between the approximation and real value is only 9 cents.

----

9) Follow example 5.5.

Time(14%, 38.2744) = 4-3 (4 years, 3 months)

----

10) Follow example 5.8.

$$RATIO = \frac{\$3,000}{\$59.19} = 50.6842$$

Use 9% because it is the closest rate to 8.9% and find the closest RATIO to 50.6842.

Time(9%, 50.6842) = 5-4 (5 years 4 month to pay back the loan)

----

11) Follow example 5.6. Look at the 4-year 5-month rows on all the tables and locate the closest RATIO to 44.0594.

APR(4-5, 44.0594) = 8.5%

----

12) Follow example 5.9.

$$RATIO = \frac{\$15,600}{\$281} = 55.5160$$

APR(7-0, 55.5160) = 12.5%

Note: True APR is 12.67%. This is due to the decimal-place accuracy of the tables.

----

13) The interest charge is the cost of borrowing the money. The total paid back on the loan is:

Total Paid = $281 x 84 = $23,604

The loan was for $15,600; therefore, the interest charged is the difference between what was originally borrowed and how much was paid back.

Interest Charged = $23,604 - $15,600 = $8,004

----

14) Follow example 5.11.

   Step 1: Principal = $88,000, Payment = $683.93, Time = 8 years

      APR = 9%

   Step 2:   Find RATIO(9%,8-0) = 68.2584

   Step 3: $88,000 - (68.2584 X $683.93) = $41,316.03

   Step 4: 12 - (68.2584 X 0.09) = 5.8567

   Step 5: $41,316.03 ÷ 5.8567 = $7,054.49

   Step 6: 12 X $7,054.49 = $84,653.88

   Unpaid Balance = $84,653.88

CHAPTER 6

MODEL SOLUTIONS

LEARN BY EXAMPLE

Most debt situations are so complex that it becomes critical to have a method for analyzing them accurately. In this chapter you will "learn by example" how to take several loans and debts and combine them into a manageable format. This "model," or scaled down replica of a larger more complicated system, represents a close approximation to the original but is more comprehensive and concise.

NEED FOR A MODEL

Before airplanes are built to full scale, small scale miniatures are created and tested in wind tunnels. These tests are performed on a small "model" plane to determine if there are any fundamental problems in the design. All types of wind conditions are created to assist engineers in determining if the plane will work as desired when it is built to full size. But just because the "model" works perfectly in the lab doesn't prove that the full scale plane will work as well; it only helps to iron out many problems before the finished product is built.

In the same way, your financial "model" will not be an exact, down-to-the-penny replica of all the original debts, but a close approximation that is easily built. It is used as a guide to determine spending and estimate savings. It can show how much debt you are in and how long it will be before you're out.

Example 6.1:

This example includes an analysis of debts and spending. The idea is not to limit spending or create a budget, but to carefully examine where the money is going.

The list of debts is as follows:

1. Credit Card 1, with a balance of $2,500, at 18.9% and payments being made at $75 per month, last due date January 7. The maximum credit limit is $2500 and the minimum payment is $75.

2. Credit Card 2, with a balance of $500, at 8.9% and payments being made at $20 per month, last due date January 28. The maximum credit limit is $4000 and the minimum payment is $20.

3. Credit Card 3, with a balance of $2,000, at 11.75% and payments being made at $60 per month, last due date January 22. The maximum credit limit is $4000 and the minimum payment is $60.

4. Car Loan, with a balance of $5,750, at 12.5% and payments being made at $200 per month, last due date December 31.

5. Store Card 1, with a balance of $800, at 19.8% and payments being made at $25 per month, last due date January 10. The maximum credit limit is $1000 and the minimum payment is $20.

6. Store Card 2, with a balance of $450, at 21% and payments being made at $25 per month, last due date January 7. The maximum credit limit is $800 and the minimum payment is $20.

ACCOUNT INFORMATION REQUIRED

Note the information needed for each loan. Most of this data can be found on the Credit Card InfoSheet with balance information located on each credit card statement. The debt in this example is short term (scheduled to be paid in full within 10 years): car loans, student loans, and credit cards.

Credit Card or Store Card
1. Outstanding Balance (principal).
2. Annual Percentage Rate (APR).
3. How much money is being paid monthly.
4. Last due date.
5. Maximum Credit Limit.
6. Minimum Payment.

Loans
1. Outstanding Balance (principal) as of today.
2. Annual Percentage Rate (APR).
3. Monthly Payment.
4. Last due date.

APPROACHING THE PROBLEM

Taken one at a time, each loan is not difficult to manage. However, understanding how the payments of one loan may affect balances of other loans, is not trivial. The approach is to create a "mathematical model" of all the loans. This "model" consolidates all debts into one "theoretical" (imaginary) loan with a single principal, interest rate and payment, thereby simplifying the problem. The math involved is no more than simple addition, subtraction, multiplication and division. Tables are provided in the appendix that eliminate the need for more complex mathematics.

ELEMENTS OF THE MODEL

Certain calculations are required to complete the model. The computations simplify the individual elements of each loan. They are:
1. Total Credit Maximum Limit
2. Total Available Credit
3. Total Debt.
4. Total Monthly Payment.
5. Dollar-Weighted Average Interest Rate.
6. Payoff Time.

TOTAL CREDIT MAXIMUM LIMIT

This represents the most money you can charge and/or cash advance if you maxed out all credit cards and lines of credit.

From example 6.1:

ACCOUNT	MAX
Credit Card 1	$2,500
Credit Card 2	$4,000
Credit Card 3	$4,000
Store Card 1	$1,000
Store Card 2	+ $800
	$12,300

Total Max = $12,300

TOTAL AVAILABLE CREDIT

This is the total amount of credit that can be utilized through cash advances or charges. What is available for your use today.

From example 6.1:

Step 1: Subtract each principal amount (outstanding balance) from the credit maximum for each account.

ACCOUNT	MAX		PRINCIPAL		DIFFERENCE
Credit Card 1	$2,500	-	$2500.00	=	$0.00
Credit Card 2	$4,000	-	$500.00	=	$3500.00
Credit Card 3	$4,000	-	$2000.00	=	$2000.00
Store Card 1	$1,000	-	$800.00	=	$200.00
Store Card 2	$800	-	$450.00	=	$350.00

Step 2: Add the DIFFERENCE column:

ACCOUNT		DIFFERENCE
Credit Card 1		$0.00
Credit Card 2		$3500.00
Credit Card 3		$2000.00
Store Card 1		$200.00
Store Card 2	+	$350.00
		$6050.00

Therefore, the total amount of available credit remaining is $6,050.00. This number, which represents the entire line of existing credit, is as important to know as the amount of money in your pocket. It is from here that you will later attempt to reduce inflated interest rates and plan future spending.

Total Available Credit = $6,050

TOTAL DEBT

This is the sum of all outstanding debt. The actual amount of money you owe creditors at this moment in time.

From example 6.1:

ACCOUNT	PRINCIPAL
Credit Card 1	$2500.00
Credit Card 2	$500.00
Credit Card 3	$2000.00
Car Loan	$5750.00
Store Card 1	$800.00
Store Card 2	+ $450.00
	$12,000.00

Total Debt = $12,000

TOTAL MONTHLY PAYMENTS

This is the sum of all monthly payments being made to these accounts.

From example 6.1:

ACCOUNT	PAYMENT
Credit Card 1	$75.00
Credit Card 2	$20.00
Credit Card 3	$60.00
Car Loan	$200.00
Store Card 1	$25.00
Store Card 2	+ $25.00
	$405.00

Total Payments = $405 per month

DOLLAR-WEIGHTED AVERAGE INTEREST RATE

Since various interest rates are being applied to each balance, it is necessary to find the Dollar-Weighted Average Interest Rate. This special interest rate is the heart of the model. It represents the true average Annual Percentage Rate applied to the entire amount of the outstanding (principal) debt. Because this rate is the Annual Percentage Rate for the Model it is abbreviated APR_M, the small "M" indicates that this is the model rate.   This is not a simple average of all the rates involved, the APR_M takes into consideration all the interest rates _and_ the amount of each balance.

The APR_M (Annual Percentage Rate of the Model) is found in 3 steps.

From example 6.1:

Step 1: To calculate the APR_M, multiply the balance of each account by the interest rate.

ACCOUNT	PRINCIPAL		INT RATE		PRINCIPAL x INT RATE
Credit Card 1	$2500.00	x	18.90	=	47250.00
Credit Card 2	$500.00	x	8.90	=	4450.00
Credit Card 3	$2000.00	x	11.75	=	23500.00
Car Loan	$5750.00	x	12.50	=	71875.00
Store Card 1	$800.00	x	19.80	=	15840.00
Store Card 2	$450.00	x	21.00	=	9450.00

Step 2: Next, add the PRINCIPAL x INT RATE column.

ACCOUNT	PRINCIPAL x INT RATE
Credit Card 1	47250.00
Credit Card 2	4450.00
Credit Card 3	23500.00
Car Loan	71875.00
Store Card 1	15840.00
Store Card 2	+ 9450.00
	172365.00

Step 3: To find the APR_M divide this total (172365.00) by the Total Debt ($12,000):

$$APR_M = \frac{172365.00}{12000.00} = 14.36$$

$APR_M \approx 14\%$ (Dollar-Weighted Average Interest Rate is approximately 14%)

The combined interest on the outstanding principal of $12,000, the sum of all current debts, is 14%, with monthly payments of $405. It is much easier to understand this single representation of these debts from example 6.1 than to manipulate the variables of all six accounts independently.

PAYOFF TIME

This number tells you how long before you are free of the total debt. Saving money on the debt will mean reducing the number of payments. The fewer payments, the less money you need to spend in interest!

In the previous chapter you learned how to solve for the Time Remaining on a loan. Follow example 5.8 with the information from the model.

What is the Time Remaining on a $12,000 loan at 14% APR with payments of $405 per month?

$$RATIO = \frac{\$12,000.00}{\$405.00} = 29.6296$$

Time(14%, 29.6296) = 3-1

The analysis on all the loans in example 6.1 concludes that the total outstanding principal is $12,000 at 14% and will be paid back in 3 years 1 month or 37 payments of $405 per month. *This statement is the model.* It is the simplification of all outstanding credit charges and loans. The next chapter presents a more concise method for calculating these results, so for now, hold off on completing the model for your debt.

CHAPTER 7

LOAN CALCULATION WORKSHEET

SIMPLER REPRESENTATION

The Loan Calculation Worksheet shows your total debt at a glance. It is a simpler way of representing the "model" that was created in the previous chapter. This worksheet takes the place of writing down the small intermediate steps in doing the calculations.

WORKSHEET USAGE SUMMARY

A summary of the columns, rows and blocks for this table are:

(A) **Account** - Name of each loan or bank.

(B) **Max** - Credit card maximum limit.

(C) **Principal** - How much is owed today.

(D) **Int Rate** - Interest rate of each loan.

(E) **Principal x Int Rate** - Principal multiplied by the interest rate.

(F) **Monthly Payment** - How much is being paid monthly toward that debt.

(G) **Open Credit** - Remaining credit.

(H) **Total Debt** - Total money owed.

(I) **Total Monthly Payments** - Total amount of money being paid monthly toward all debts.

(J) **APR$_M$** - Dollar-Weighted Average Interest Rate of the total debt (Average Annual Percentage Rate for the Model).

(K) **RATIO** - Total Principal divided by Total Monthly Payments.

(L) **Payoff Time** - Time Remaining to pay off debt.

　　　TOTALS - Sum of all the numbers of a particular column.

EXAMPLE WORKSHEET

By following the procedures and steps outlined when analyzing example 6.1, the worksheet is filled in as follows:

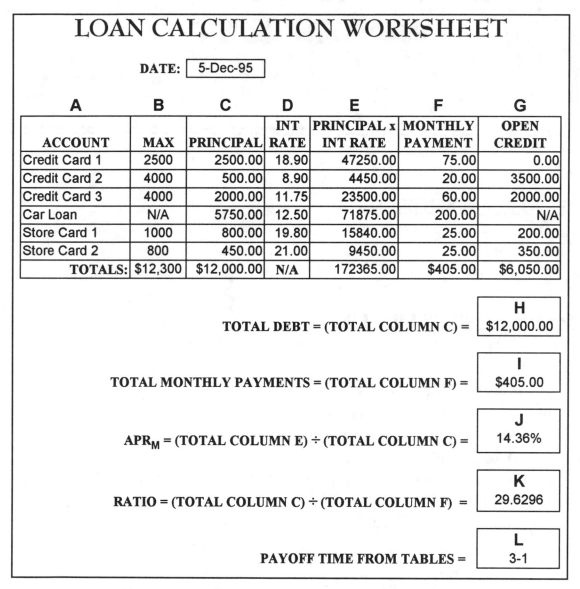

LOAN CALCULATION WORKSHEET

DATE: 5-Dec-95

	A	B	C	D	E	F	G
	ACCOUNT	MAX	PRINCIPAL	INT RATE	PRINCIPAL x INT RATE	MONTHLY PAYMENT	OPEN CREDIT
	Credit Card 1	2500	2500.00	18.90	47250.00	75.00	0.00
	Credit Card 2	4000	500.00	8.90	4450.00	20.00	3500.00
	Credit Card 3	4000	2000.00	11.75	23500.00	60.00	2000.00
	Car Loan	N/A	5750.00	12.50	71875.00	200.00	N/A
	Store Card 1	1000	800.00	19.80	15840.00	25.00	200.00
	Store Card 2	800	450.00	21.00	9450.00	25.00	350.00
	TOTALS:	$12,300	$12,000.00	N/A	172365.00	$405.00	$6,050.00

TOTAL DEBT = (TOTAL COLUMN C) =

H
$12,000.00

TOTAL MONTHLY PAYMENTS = (TOTAL COLUMN F) =

I
$405.00

APR_M **= (TOTAL COLUMN E) ÷ (TOTAL COLUMN C) =**

J
14.36%

RATIO = (TOTAL COLUMN C) ÷ (TOTAL COLUMN F) =

K
29.6296

PAYOFF TIME FROM TABLES =

L
3-1

Figure 7.1: Loan Calculation Worksheet with data from example 6.1.

Once the worksheet is completed Blocks H, I, J and L will contain the model of all your debts.

COMPLETING THE WORKSHEET

Make a few photocopies of the blank worksheet shown at the end of this chapter. Using the example worksheet and Chapter 6 as a guide, take the information from your loans and complete the Loan Calculation Worksheet by following these steps:

1. Fill in Account (A), Max (B), Principal (C), Interest Rate (D) and Monthly Payment (F) Columns.

2. Subtract Principal (C) from Max (B) to find Open Credit for each account and enter result in Column G.

3. Multiply the Principal (C) by the Interest Rate (D) and enter results into Column E.

4. Add Columns B, C, E, F, and G and place the totals in the TOTALS row.

5. Enter the Total of Column C into Block H.

6. Enter the Total of Column F into Block I.

7. Calculate the APR_M by dividing the total of Column E by the total of Column C and enter result into Block J.

8. Calculate the RATIO by dividing the total of Column C by the total of Column F and enter result into Block K.

9. Look up the PAYOFF TIME using the RATIO and the Time-Remaining Tables in the Appendix and enter into Block L.

BLANK LOAN CALCULATION WORKSHEET

LOAN CALCULATION WORKSHEET

DATE: [   ]

A	B	C	D	E	F	G
ACCOUNT	**MAX**	**PRINCIPAL**	**INT RATE**	**PRINCIPAL x INT RATE**	**MONTHLY PAYMENT**	**OPEN CREDIT**
TOTALS:			N/A			

TOTAL DEBT = (TOTAL COLUMN C) = [H]

TOTAL MONTHLY PAYMENTS = (TOTAL COLUMN F) = [I]

APR_M = (TOTAL COLUMN E) ÷ (TOTAL COLUMN C) = [J]

RATIO = (TOTAL COLUMN C) ÷ (TOTAL COLUMN F) = [K]

PAYOFF TIME FROM TABLES = [L]

CHAPTER 8

PAYMENT SCHEDULE WORKSHEET

In the previous chapter you calculated principal, interest rate, monthly payments and payoff time of all your debt by creating a model. The goal of this book is to assist you in reducing these payments, which in turn, will save money. However, to be more accurate in the modeling of your particular situation, you need to examine more detailed information about your general spending habits.

So far you have only looked at debt, which is paid from some source of income. To fully "model" your entire financial life you must explore income and other monthly payments that are not related to credit cards and loans. Once a complete representation of your periodical expenditures is realized, you can begin making intelligent choices that save money on interest payments.

All debt must eventually be paid for with income — net income. Therefore, it is important to know the amount of money available for handling all your debt payments and payments for other obligations.

INCOME

Since most people are paid weekly and can manage money more easily when using weekly income figures, it is important to investigate how bills are handled when planning bank deposits and spending. If you already know what you earn weekly then you have the answer, but if some or all of your income is paid monthly, biweekly or in some other manner there is an extra step to finding your net weekly income. This is the weekly net pay (after taxes and deductions) — the money at your disposal.

Example 8.1:

How much per week is $2,028 per month (this is take-home money, also known as net income)?

Solution 8.1:

Since there are 12 months in a year the total annual net income is:

$$12 \times \$2,028 = \$24,336 \text{ per year}$$

Since there are 52 weeks in the year, dollars per week equals:

$$\frac{\$24,336}{52} = \$468 \text{ per week}$$

For the purpose of completing example 6.1 (model), $468 per week will be the amount used to finish the analysis.

OTHER MONTHLY PAYMENTS

You already have information about debts from the Loan Calculation Worksheet. Now you need to know other periodic payment data.

The categories included are:
1. Auto Insurance
2. Food
3. Water/Sewer
4. Natural Gas/Oil
5. Phone
6. Electric
7. Mortgage or Rent
8. Any other known periodic payments

An attempt must be made to estimate unknown or potential expenses. As long as you know payments are due in any area, especially if they are recurring, they must be accounted for when you analyze your debt. Phone charges are a good example. To get a good estimate, average the last 6 months of your bills.

Phone Charges:

July	-	$100.00
August	-	$90.00
September	-	$60.00
October	-	$70.00
November	-	$80.00
December	-	$80.00
TOTAL		**$480.00**

$$\text{Average} = \frac{\$480.00}{6} = \$80 \text{ per month}$$

Estimate the monthly expenses that fall into these categories. To complete example 6.1 these categories and expenses will be used:

Auto Insurance	-	$70.00
Food	-	$200.00
Heat	-	$90.00
Rent	-	$750.00
Health Club	-	$50.00

Next, estimate normal spending that does not fit into the previously mentioned categories. The dollars spent in these categories are the hardest to determine. These might include:

1. Automobile Services/Repairs
2. Charity
3. Clothing
4. Entertainment
5. Gambling
6. Gasoline
7. Gifts
8. Home Repair
9. Insurance (Life, Medical, etc.)
10. Lunches & Dining Out
11. Medical
12. Misc.
13. Office Supplies and Stamps
14. Subscriptions

The more information you can locate concerning these not-so-obvious payments, the more accurate the model. **To continue with example 6.1 we will estimate the amount of these categories combined to total $200 per month.**

EXAMPLE PAYMENT SCHEDULE

With a more accurate spending model the Payment Schedule Worksheet for example 6.1 is filled in as follows:

PAYMENT SCHEDULE

DATE: | Dec 5

Weekly: | $425.77 | **A**

Minimum Weekly: | $423.46 | **B**

Left over weekly: | $42.23 | **C**

Available Credit: | $6,050.00 | **D**

E	**F**	**G**	**H**
ACCOUNT	**DUE DATE**	**MONTHLY PAYMENT**	**MINIMUM PAYMENT**
Auto Insurance	Jan 1	70.00	70.00
Food		200.00	200.00
Heat	Jan 22	90.00	90.00
Rent	Jan 15	750.00	750.00
Health Club	Jan 15	50.00	50.00
Phone	Jan 11	80.00	80.00
Spending		200.00	200.00
Credit Card 1	Jan 7	75.00	75.00
Credit Card 2	Jan 28	20.00	20.00
Credit Card 3	Jan 22	60.00	60.00
Car Loan	Dec 31	200.00	200.00
Store Card 1	Jan 10	25.00	20.00
Store Card 2	Jan 7	25.00	20.00
TOTALS:	N/A	**$1,845.00**	**$1,835.00**

Figure 8.1: Payment Schedule for example 6.1.

WORKSHEET USAGE SUMMARY

Make a few photocopies of the blank Payment Schedule located at the end of this chapter. Fill in the Payment Schedule with your information by following this procedure:

1. Fill in Account (E), Due Date (F), Monthly Payment (G) and Minimum Payment (H) Columns. The information from the Loan Calculation Worksheet provides the debt information. The Due Date Column is the due date from your most recent statement.

2. Add the Monthly Payment (G) and Minimum Payment (H) Columns and enter the result in the Totals row.

3. Find the Weekly cost of your debt by multiplying the total for Column G by 12 then divide by 52, Weekly $= \dfrac{\$1,845 \times 12}{52} = \$425.77$ and enter result in Block A.

4. Find the Minimum Weekly cost of your debt by multiplying the total for Column H by 12 then divide by 52, Weekly $= \dfrac{\$1,835 \times 12}{52} = \$423.46$ and enter result in Block B.

5. Subtract the Weekly payment (Block A, $425.77) from total weekly income ($468.00 from example 6.1) and enter the result ($42.23) in Block C. This represents what is left over weekly from all spending and payments, and could be considered savings.

6. From the Loan Calculation Worksheet (figure 7.1), find the total of Column G and enter into Block D.

So far you have done quite a bit of work by completing the Loan Calculation Worksheet and the Payment Schedule. You know the Loan Calculation Worksheet created the model of debt needed to simplify all the loans. The Payment Schedule Worksheet is the actual guide to follow when paying your bills.

When you pay bills you know which ones are due, when and in what amount by following your Payment Schedule. Also, you know how much money is required to fulfill your lifestyle. For example, block A (Weekly), represents how much money you need on a weekly basis to pay your bills when they become due. To pay all the bills listed from example 6.1, figure 8.1, $425.77 must be deposited in the bank every week. If this is done, then the total $1,845.00 (Total Monthly Payment) is available when the monthly statements arrive.

SUMMARY OF INFORMATION FROM PAYMENT SCHEDULE:

1. **Block A** - *Weekly* - Displays the weekly deposit that must be made in order to pay all bills listed on the worksheet.

2. **Block B** - *Minimum Weekly* - If you decided to make the minimum payments on all your bills this is the lowest amount you need per week to make those payments. The example worksheet shows the minimum payment as $423.46, which leaves almost no flexibility from the payments that are being made already. Ultimately, you want to be paying more than the Minimum Payment so you have some flexibility between the Minimum Payment and the desired payment.

3. **Block C** - *Left over weekly* - This is how much money remains after you have made the correct deposit that ensures you can pay all bills on time. This is money that you can spend or save; money that you can truly enjoy on a weekly basis as disposable income.

4. **Block D** - *Available Credit* - This is also a measure of flexibility. The more available credit you have, the more options for refinancing you have. This amount can be quite high and should not be abused by impulse spending.

BLANK PAYMENT SCHEDULE

PAYMENT SCHEDULE

DATE: [ ]

Weekly: [ ] **A**

Minimum Weekly: [ ] **B**

Left over weekly: [ ] **C**

Available Credit: [ ] **D**

E ACCOUNT	F DUE DATE	G MONTHLY PAYMENT	H MINIMUM PAYMENT
TOTALS:	N/A		

CHAPTER 9

CREDIT SOLUTIONS

GOALS

So far you have analyzed spending and debt with no consideration of limiting any expenditures — budgeting. Getting organized and tracking your debt with the worksheets makes you more aware of your spending habits. This book is not designed to make budgeting suggestions; the worksheets are created as a guide to paying off debt.

The results from the Payment Schedule Worksheet for example 6.1 indicate that if $425.77 is deposited weekly all bills and spending are satisfied. Now that the model is complete, it is time to start listing possible goals.

1. Pay all debts back as quickly as possible.
2. Cut spending in categories that are flexible, e.g., groceries, dining out, entertainment, etc.
3. Buy necessary new items that add to your debt.
4. Start a savings account.

To achieve these goals you need money, and the first place to start looking for money is by saving on interest payments. There should be some areas that can be improved. The only ways to save money on your interest charges and pay debt back faster are:

1. Lower your interest rates.
2. Pay more money towards debt.
3. Make higher payments to higher interest debts — transfer balances.

That's it! This is a mathematical reality just as gravity is a physical reality. The question is, how to go about doing it.

LOWERING YOUR INTEREST RATES

The first area to examine is lowering your Dollar-Weighted Average Interest Rate (APR_M). To lower the overall rate, you must transfer the higher interest debt to lower interest credit cards or loans. If you made payments to your creditors on time you should have more lower interest rate cards and options. If not, work with what you have and take advantage of any good offers received.

Example 6.1 revisited

Notice that $3,500 is available on Credit Card 2 at 8.9% (figure 7.1), this is considerably less than the APR_M 14.36%. Also, $2,000 is available on Credit Card 3 at 11.75%, this too is lower than the APR_M.

The total cash available on the lower rate cards is $5,500. This money should be advanced and sent to the highest interest cards. *BEWARE! Some banks charge a higher rate for cash advances than charges. You must call the 800 number on your card and make sure you're getting a low rate for cash advances.*

The highest interest rate debt listed on the Loan Calculation Worksheet is Store Card 2, which has a balance of $450. Paying this off leaves $5,050. The next highest rate is Store Card 1, with a balance of $800. Paying this off leaves $4,250. Credit Card 1 is paid next with a balance of $2,500. This leaves $1,750, which is paid toward the Car Loan. Although the Car Loan's interest rate is less than the APR_M it is <u>still higher</u> than the available credit rates. Figure 9.1 describes the transfers.

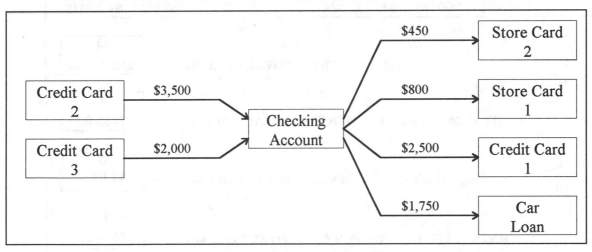

Figure 9.1: Transferring balances.

PAYING A LITTLE MORE

According to the Payment Schedule, there is approximately $42.23 per week remaining — $183.00 per month. Taking a small sum of money, say $80, and applying that toward the debt also reduces the total interest payments. For example 6.1, $80 extra is applied to the highest rated loan after all transfers are complete — this is the Car Loan which has a 12.5% rate.

Since balances changed, minimum payments on Credit Cards 2 and 3 increased to $120 per month after the transfers are complete. However, since Store Card 1 and Store Card 2 are paid off from the transfers, the payments that otherwise were made there are applied to Credit Cards 1,2, 3 and the Car Loan.

NEW LOAN CALCULATION WORKSHEET

When the transfers are complete, create a new Loan Calculation Worksheet, which reflects the updated balances. The following is the new worksheet for example 6.1.

LOAN CALCULATION WORKSHEET

TODAY'S DATE: 5-Dec-95

A	B	C	D	E	F	G
ACCOUNT	MAX	PRINCIPAL	INT RATE	PRINCIPAL x INT RATE	MONTHLY PAYMENT	OPEN CREDIT
Credit Card 1	2500	0.00	18.90	0.00	0.00	2500.00
Credit Card 2	4000	4000.00	8.90	35600.00	120.00	0.00
Credit Card 3	4000	4000.00	11.75	47000.00	120.00	0.00
Car Loan	N/A	4000.00	12.50	50000.00	245.00	N/A
Store Card 1	1000	0.00	19.80	0.00	0.00	1000.00
Store Card 2	800	0.00	21.00	0.00	0.00	800.00
TOTALS:	$12,300	$12,000.00	N/A	132600.00	$485.00	$4,300.00

TOTAL DEBT = (TOTAL COLUMN C) =

H
$12,000.00

TOTAL MONTHLY PAYMENTS = (TOTAL COLUMN F) =

I
$485.00

APR_M = (TOTAL COLUMN E) ÷ (TOTAL COLUMN C) =

J
11.05%

RATIO = (TOTAL COLUMN C) ÷ (TOTAL COLUMN F) =

K
24.7423

PAYOFF TIME (YEARS) FROM TABLES =

L
2-4

Figure 9.2: New Loan Calculation Worksheet

Notice how much lower the APR_M is once the calculations are complete. Without applying for any new loans or getting any new credit, the APR_M from the example dropped from 14.36% to 11.05%. This is the same as refinancing your entire debt at a rate 3.31% lower, without having to go through the bank lending process.

Next, look up the new payoff time. This dropped from 3 years, 1 month (37 months) to 2 years, 4 months (28 months). That knocks 9 months of time off paying the debt back!

CALCULATING SAVINGS

Nine months of the original payments of $405 per month do not need to be paid. This is a savings of $3,645. But, there are extra payments of $80 per month toward the debt for 28 months, which adds up to $2,240. Therefore, the total saved is:

$$\$3,645 - \$2,240 = \$1,405$$

Keep in mind that any savings is in the form of interest payments. In this case by rearranging the debt, $1,405 that would have been spent on interest is saved. All savings are interest savings because the original principal must always be paid back. Therefore if you can pay the debt off earlier it means you paid the entire original principal plus the finance charges with fewer payments. Another way to calculate savings is by finding the total amount of money needed to pay back each case:

Example 9.1:
Find the savings after transferring the balances for example 6.1.

Solution 9.1:

Case 1: Original payment plan from figure 7.1.

　　　　37 payments of $405 add up to $14,985.

Case 2: New Loan Calculation Worksheet after transfers figure 9.2.

　　　　28 payments of $485 add up to $13,580.

　　　　Savings = $14,985 - $13,580 = $1,405.

That's not too bad for giving up only $18.50 a week and taking the time to examine and manage the debt.

In the previous example of moving debt to lower interest rate cards it was assumed that the cash advance interest rate was equivalent to the interest rate of the original debt. Some bank cards, however, charge a higher rate for cash advances than for charges. **How do you transfer debt from one card to another if the cash advance rate is higher than the charge rate?**

No problem. Charge all your normal spending to the card with the lower charge rate. Then save the cash you would have spent on those items and use it to pay the high rate card. This is equivalent to getting a free cash advance at a lower rate.

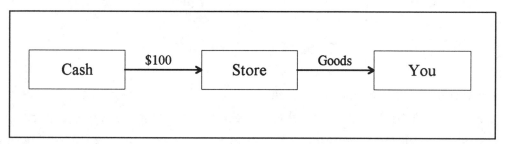

Figure 9.3: Buying with cash.

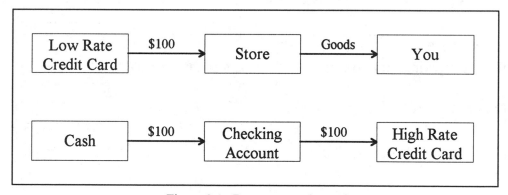

Figure 9.4: Buy, save, and transfer.

You must be careful to follow through on this spending plan or it will put you into more debt. Be disciplined. Keep that money in the checking account and pay it to the proper banks. While you do this there will be more cash in your accounts. Remember that this cash is meant to reduce your debt and is not available for care-free spending!

NEW PAYMENT SCHEDULE

Next, you need to create a new Payment Schedule and closely examine the Minimum Payment column. The example is shown below:

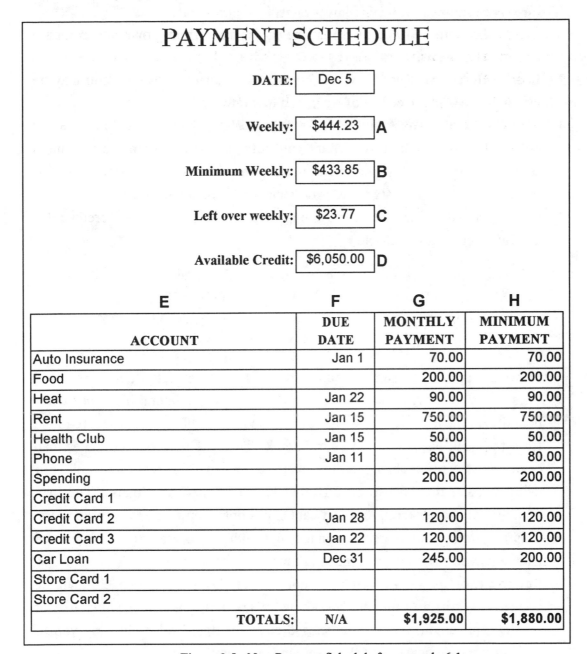

PAYMENT SCHEDULE

DATE: Dec 5

Weekly: $444.23 **A**

Minimum Weekly: $433.85 **B**

Left over weekly: $23.77 **C**

Available Credit: $6,050.00 **D**

E	F	G	H
ACCOUNT	**DUE DATE**	**MONTHLY PAYMENT**	**MINIMUM PAYMENT**
Auto Insurance	Jan 1	70.00	70.00
Food		200.00	200.00
Heat	Jan 22	90.00	90.00
Rent	Jan 15	750.00	750.00
Health Club	Jan 15	50.00	50.00
Phone	Jan 11	80.00	80.00
Spending		200.00	200.00
Credit Card 1			
Credit Card 2	Jan 28	120.00	120.00
Credit Card 3	Jan 22	120.00	120.00
Car Loan	Dec 31	245.00	200.00
Store Card 1			
Store Card 2			
TOTALS:	**N/A**	**$1,925.00**	**$1,880.00**

Figure 9.5: New Payment Schedule for example 6.1.

The only financial flexibility you have is the difference between the Minimum Weekly Payments and net income. If your minimum weekly payment ever exceeds your weekly net income, you will go into debt every week forever. In this case the total flexibility is: $468.00 - $433.85 = $34.15 ($468 is the total weekly net income used in example 6.1).

FINDING LOWER RATES

It is obvious that lowering the combined interest rate of all the debt saves a considerable amount of money. The problem might be finding banks that offer lower rates. Here are some sources for finding lower rates.

1. **Credit Card InfoSheet** - Look at the cards you currently own and compare interest rates as with example 6.1.

2. **Credit Offer InfoSheet** - What offers do you currently have? You may be pre-approved for a nice line of credit at a low rate.

3. **Local papers** - The Asbury Park Press, a local paper in my area, periodically publishes a list of the lowest credit card rates in the nation in their business section. Your local paper might publish this list as well. Barron's also publishes a list of low rate cards as do many other money magazines.

4. **Buying a list** - There are some groups that sell lists of the best credit rates and terms currently available.

Bankcard Holders of America	CardTrak
524 Branch Drive	PO Box 1700
Salem, VA 24153	Frederick, MD 21702
(540) 389-5445	(800) 344-7714

6. **Secured Loans** - Usually secured loans offer lower rates than unsecured ones, for obvious reasons. The lender can seize the collateral if the borrower defaults on the loan. If you own a car you might be able to get a secured loan from the bank using your car as collateral. This rate may also be lower than other credit cards enabling you to lower the combined interest rate of all your debt by using this loan to payoff other higher interest rate loans. The loan might be of shorter term; for older cars banks only lend money for three years. This may raise your monthly payment, but with the lower rate and increased payments you save money in the long run.

7. **Second Mortgages** - If you have equity in your house (you owe less than the house is worth) you may be able to get a good rate with an equity line of credit. This credit line could be closed-ended or open-ended allowing you to cash advance money against the equity in your home.

8. **401K** - There are certain conditions for borrowing money from your retirement plan, but the low interest rate makes this very attractive.

9. **Family and Friends** - They may be your least expensive source of credit and possibly the easiest to deal with. Make sure you honor this loan and put it first on your list of payments. You do not want to ruin any relationships over money.

ACCURACY OF MODEL

A model is a tool. The financial model built using the combined interest rate of all debt (Dollar-Weighted Average Interest Rate) is a method of condensing many different loans into one manageable form. The most important aspect of this model is its ability to predict the payoff time of all debts involved. The payoff time computed using the Loan Calculation Worksheet is not exact but a close approximation. The true payoff time and combined interest rate differs slightly depending how you chose to make payments for each individual loan.

To calculate the true payoff time for every payment strategy is an arduous task, especially if done frequently. Calculating the information in the Loan Calculation Worksheet is relatively simple. That's the reason for using the model; it is an easy way to provide accurate and useful information about multiple loans.

For the sake of completeness, we will examine the true numbers for the latest Loan Calculation Worksheet (figure 9.2). This worksheet represents the best arrangement possible that reduces the combined interest rate from example 6.1.

The next strategy that saves money is the method of payment to each loan. **Sending the most money to the highest interest rate cards is a fundamental of effective debt management.** These high rate cards are charging the most interest for loans. Eliminating them as quickly as possible saves money!

From the Loan Calculation Worksheet (figure 9.2) notice that there are only three debts remaining; credit cards 2 and 3 plus the car loan. There are many ways to spend the $485 per month between these debts but we will only look at the three extreme cases to determine the true payoff time. These three cases represent the most effective, least effective and most realistic ways to pay back the debt.

Payment Method 1:

The most efficient way to spend the $485 per month is sending the whole payment to the highest interest rate loan — the car loan. Eventually when this loan is paid off you would send the $485 to credit card 3 and when that is paid off the money would be sent to credit card 2. The true payoff time in this case is 27.92 payments or a total of:

$$27.92 \times \$485 = \$13,541.20$$

This is the cheapest and fastest way to pay the entire balance. It would be nice if other banks would wait until you're done paying off the more expensive loans first, but the reality is that this method cannot be put to practical use.

Payment Method 2:

This is the worst way to go about making payments. This is the opposite of Payment Method 1, which is paying the lowest rate debts back first then continuing to apply that money until you get to the highest rate debts. In this case the true payoff time is 28.51 payments or a total of:

$$28.51 \times \$485 = \$13,827.35$$

Payment Method 3:

This is a realistic method which takes into consideration the fact that there are Minimum Payments that prevent using methods 1 and 2. They are the theoretical best and worst case. Using Payment Method 3, you would pay the most money to the highest interest rate cards but still pay the Minimum Payment on the lower rate cards.

As the balances of the lower rate cards become smaller, so does the Minimum Payment. As this happens, you continue sending the Minimum Payment to those cards, keeping the total payment that is being applied to all the debt at $485 per month. As the highest interest rate loans get paid off, the money that was sent to these loans is applied to the remaining loans that have the highest rate. The true payoff time for this method is 28.07 payments which is a total of:

$$28.07 \times \$485 = \$13,613.95$$

That is the best that can be done with the example problem.

Example 6.1 (Model)

Compare these different methods to the model represented by figure 9.2. The payoff time from the model is 2 years, 4 months which is 28 months. That is a total of:

$$28 \times \$485 = \$13,580.00$$

Here is the summary:

Payment Method	Total Paid Back	Difference from Model
Model	$13,580.00	N/A
Method 1	$13,541.20	($38.80)*
Method 2	$13,827.35	$247.35
Method 3	$13,613.95	$33.95

Table 9.1: Summary of Methods

Numbers in parentheses indicate the difference is less than the model.

Notice how close each of the methods are to the model. Take careful note of Method 3, the one that is actually used. The true payoff total is only $33.95 from the model. So after paying back $13,613.95 in 2 years, 4 months the model is only off 0.25%, well within an acceptable estimate.

LOWEST POSSIBLE MONTHLY PAYMENTS

The Minimum Payment that can be made to a loan should not be lower than the cost of that month's interest. If the payment is lower than the interest, you go into debt forever; this is formally known as Negative Amortization.

Therefore, the absolute minimum payment for example 6.1 is:

$$\text{Principal x } \frac{\text{Interest Rate}}{12} = \$12,000 \text{ x } \frac{0.1105}{12} = \$110.50$$

The actual payment schedule calls for $485 a month, an amount that exceeds the monthly interest. If the amount being paid back is less than $110.50, then the RATIO would not exist on the Time-Remaining Tables even if the time of the tables are extended forever. This is because any amount less than $110.50 doesn't pay off that period's interest; i.e., if you were paying $100, then $10.50 would be added on to the principal of the debt. As the debt grows, so does the interest. This domino effect makes the principal grow forever.

If you are borrowing against your credit just to pay the bills, your time is limited by your credit maximum. You will be able to cash-advance money up to your limit and then the only alternative is bankruptcy. This is a situation you must avoid; you can easily do so by paying more toward the loans and transferring high interest rate debt to credit lines with lower interest rates.

HOW MUCH MORE DEBT CAN YOU TAKE

Continuing with example 6.1, the next question asked is: *How much more can you spend (how much more debt can example 6.1 handle)?* There is $4,300 in available credit, but is there enough money to make payments on that, even at the minimum?

All credit cards have a Minimum Payment Policy. The Minimum Payment is usually equal to the entire balance divided by some number, but not less than a dollar minimum. A conservative Minimum Payment Policy is:

The Minimum Payment is equal to the balance divided by 33 but not less than $20.

The divisor (33) varies from card to card; some are as high as 50. The higher that number is, the lower the Minimum Payment.

Using this policy, the Minimum Payment for new debt is equal to the available money weekly (after all obligations are paid) multiplied by 143. In the Loan Calculation Worksheet (figure 9.2) there is $34.15 per week remaining from the net income of $468. If the Minimum Payment is used on the existing debt. The approximate debt that this can pay for is:

$$\$34.15 \times 143 = \$4,883.45$$

If that worksheet gained $4,883.45 of debt there would be no money left over every week to be used for making payments. I don't recommend going to this limit because if something does come up which needs financial attention, you will be unable to respond since all your money is tied up in paying back debt at minimum payments. This calculation gives you an idea of what your theoretical maximum is and alerts you to watch your charges and stay far away from reaching that number.

CHAPTER 10

CHOOSING THE BEST CREDIT CARD: Fees and Effects

Here's the question:

Which of the following credit cards should you use if you need to borrow $4,000 cash: one card has a rate of 14.9% and no annual fee; the other has a 11.9% rate and a $50 annual fee?

The answer is, you need more information.

This is an important question for at least two reasons. First, you want to save the most money possible when using credit. Second, there are so many credit cards available, each with different terms and conditions, that you need a method to compare them.

Deciding the best card to use for balance transfers and cash advances is imperative. Taking the time to figure out which card offers the least cost for your specific borrowing needs is the easiest way to save. It is like shopping for anything else, but you can do it at home with the information provided in this book.

FEES

Before tackling the original problem it is necessary to understand what affects the comparison. What mainly influences the cost of borrowing are the fees. These fees include but may not be limited to:

1. Annual fees.
2. Cash advance fees.
3. Interest rates.

ANNUAL FEE

Many credit cards charge a fixed fee annually. This charge can be from zero to $100 or more depending on the bank and other conditions on the account, such as interest rate, services provided, or payment terms. One thing is certain, the annual fee can make borrowing money more expensive.

CASH ADVANCE FEES

Not only are annual fees charged but there may also be cash advance fees. This fee is charged when you take the money from a cash machine, bank, or write a check against your credit line.

There are usually three factors that determine the cash advance fee:
1. Percentage of the amount advanced.
2. Minimum charge.
3. Maximum charge.

An example cash advance fee policy:

Cash advance fee will be 2% of the amount, not less than $2 and not greater than $20.

This policy has previously (Chapter 4) been represented by the following notation:

$$\$2 < 2\% < \$20$$

The steps required to calculate the cash advance fee with this policy are:

1. Find 2% of the amount advanced.
2. Compare the 2% figure and the minimum amount of $2. If 2% is less than $2, then the fee is $2.
3. Compare the 2% figure and maximum amount of $20. If 2% is greater than $20, then the fee is $20.
4. If the 2% figure is greater than $2 and less than $20, then the 2% figure is the fee.

> **Example 10.1:**
> What is the cash advance fee charged when borrowing $5,000 when the fee policy is $2 < 2% < $20?
>
> **Solution:**
> **Step 1:** Find 2% of $5,000.
>
> $$(.02) \times (\$5,000) = \$100$$
>
> **Step 2:** Compare to the minimum and maximum charges.
>
> *Since $100 is greater than the $20 maximum, the cash advance fee is $20.*

Some banks might have a minimum charge and no maximum charge. Others may have a flat fee for cash advances, i.e., a set fee no matter what the amount advanced. Still others might charge nothing at all if you transfer the balance of another credit card to their bank. **Some banks will even pay you to transfer balances!**

> **Example 10.2:**
> What is the cash advance fee charged when borrowing $4,000 when the fee policy is $2 < 2%?
>
> **Solution:**
> **Step 1:** Find 2% of $4,000.
>
> $$(.02) \times (\$4,000) = \$80$$
>
> **Step 2:** Compare to the minimum charges.
>
> *Since there is no maximum amount (ceiling), on the amount that can be charged the cash advance fee is $80.*

INTEREST RATE

The APR (Annual Percentage Rate) charged is the most critical factor in determining which loans and credit cards are superior. In general the lower rate is best, but there are many exceptions. **Be careful, some credit cards charge a higher rate for cash advances than for purchases.** Check your monthly statement or credit card agreement to find out what the policy is for interest rates as they apply to advances. This information should be recorded on the Credit Card InfoSheet.

WHAT TO COMPARE

Many parameters must be considered when determining which credit card or loan to accept. Every comparison is unique and must be analyzed carefully. The parameters to be taken into account are:

1. Annual fees.
2. Cash advance fees.
3. Interest rate (APR).
4. Whether the interest rate is fixed or variable.
5. Amount (principal) of money that is needed.
6. Monthly payment.
7. Number of months you will make those payments.
8. Short term financial plans.

There are many ways to compare and analyze how these variables affect each credit card being considered. We will use a future value analysis. **The Future Value is the dollar amount of the unpaid loan after a certain number of payments.** The credit card or loan that is paid off the most, has the lowest unpaid balance (future value), in the time frame considered, is the better deal. In Chapter 5, "Calculating the Unpaid Balance", you calculated the future value of a loan. You can use the same techniques presented in that section to do loan comparisons but since some new conditions are needed, a new technique and new table are also needed.

The example comparisons in this chapter use a one-year (12 payments) time frame. Using a one-year period is necessary because annual fees are charged once a year. The analysis can be done for more than one year by repeating the same techniques.

To fairly assess the value of each particular loan, some conditions must be defined and held constant while making comparisons.

Conditions:
1. All money is cash advanced or transferred from one account to another.
2. The money advanced for each loan in the comparison must be the same.
3. Cash advance fees are charged immediately to the account when money is borrowed.
4. The Monthly Payment for each loan must be the same. If you can afford to pay one card a certain amount you can just as easily pay it to another.
5. The time period of comparison will be one year (12 payments).

Let's begin by looking at the original question in greater detail.

Which of the following credit cards should you use if you need to borrow $4,000 cash: one card has a rate of 14.9% and no annual fee; the other has a 11.9% rate and a $50 annual fee?

It was originally stated that there was not enough information available to solve this problem. After reading the considerations and conditions necessary to make a valid comparison, it is apparent the missing information is:

1. How much will be paid back monthly.
2. Number of months that payment will be made.
3. Short term financial plans.
4. Whether there are any cash advance fees.
5. Whether the interest rate is fixed or variable.

You might want to know what the minimum payment is in order to determine how much to pay back monthly. For example, if the minimum payment is $123.00, but you are capable of paying more and decide on $130.00 per month. This payment will be made every month for one year, to whichever card you use. Remember, this is one of the conditions that must be true for analysis to be fair and accurate.

Financial plans are important when making comparisons. If you are plan to transfer the balance to another loan soon, you need to look at different aspects of the comparison. If you change your planned payments, this also affects the results of the analysis. **The only way to ensure that you make the right choice is to do what you planned and follow through.**

The problem never stated if there are any cash advance fees or if the rates are fixed. For the purpose of completing this example there are no cash advance fees for either card and interest rates are fixed.

Now that you have all the information necessary to begin the comparison analysis, you can restate the question more precisely:

Example 10.4:
I need to borrow $4,000. I can afford to spend $130 per month to pay back the debt. I will make $130 payments every month for one year. I have a choice between two credit cards; neither charge a cash advance fee. Both cards have a fixed interest rate for one year. The first card has an interest rate of 14.9% and no annual fee. The second

card has an interest rate of 11.9% and a $50 annual fee. Which card should I use if I want to have paid back the most money toward that debt after exactly 12 payments?

It is important to define the problem as close to the true situation as possible. The comparison is valid <u>only</u> if the information provided in the question is accurate.

BALANCE & PAYMENT FACTOR TABLE

The Balance and Payment Factor Tables in the appendix provide information about the future value of money at different rates. You need to utilize these factors when comparing different credit cards.

The two factors are:
1. Balance Factor.
2. Payment Factor.

Follow example 10.3 and learn how to use the Balance & Payment Factor Table.

Example 10.3:

What are the Balance and Payment Factors for an interest rate of 13.6%?

Solution:

Step 1: Go to the Balance & Payment Factors table in the appendix.

Step 2: Find 13.6% in the column.

Step 3: The factors are located next to the interest rate in the appropriate columns (page 133).

Balance Factor = 1.1448
Payment Factor = 12.7770

FUTURE VALUE COMPARISON

The Future Value Comparison computes how much principal remains on the loan after one year. Again, the loan with the lowest balance is the better choice.

Steps to doing the Future Value Comparison:

1. Calculate all cash advance fees and annual fees, then add these amounts to the principal needed.
2. Find the Balance and Payment Factors for the interest rate.
3. Calculate the Future Value by using the following formula:
   Future Value = (Principal x Balance Factor) - (Payment x Payment Factor)

Solution 10.4:
PART 1: Solve for the Future Value of the loan if credit card 1 is used.

Step 1: Calculate all cash advance fees and annual fees.
This card had none.

Step 2: Find the Balance and Payment Factor for 14.9% in the table (page 134).
Balance Factor = 1.1596
Payment Factor = 12.8544

Step 3: Compute the Future Value of the $4,000 using the Factors.
Future Value = (Principal x Balance Factor) - (Payment x Payment Factor)
Future Value = ($4,000 x 1.1596) - ($130 x 12.8544)
Future Value = ($4,638.40) - ($1,671.07)

Future Value = $2,967.33

This means that after making $130 payment for 12 months the balance after the 12th payment is $2,967.33.

PART 2: Solve for the Future Value of the loan if credit card 2 is used.

Step 1: Calculate all cash advance fees and annual fees.
This card has an annual fee of $50. After $4,000 is taken from the account, $50 is charged. Adding this fee to the original money borrowed creates an initial loan principal of $4,050 ($4,000 plus the $50 annual fee).

Step 2: Find the Balance and Payment Factor for 11.9% in the table (page 133).
Balance Factor = 1.1257
Payment Factor = 12.6766

Step 3: Compute the Future Value of the $4,050 using the Factors.

Future Value = (Principal × Balance Factor) - (Payment × Payment Factor)

Future Value = ($4,050 × 1.1257) - ($130 × 12.6766)

Future Value = ($4,559.09) - ($1,647.96)

$$Future\ Value = \$2,911.13$$

This means that after making $130 payments for 12 months, the balance remaining after the 12th payment is $2,911.13.

The 11.9% card is the better card in this specific case, because the Future Value of the amount borrowed is less than the Future Value of the 14.9% card. The amount saved over the course of the year is the difference between the Future Values.

$$Total\ Saved = \$2,967.33 - \$2,911.13 = \$56.20$$

$56.20 is not bad for solving a math problem!

Even though the 11.9% card has a lower Future Value at the end of the year, that doesn't mean it is the best at every month during the year. Remember, the 11.9% card started out with a higher balance because of the annual fee. There was some point (cross-over point) during the year that the balance of the 11.9% card became lower than the balance of the 14.9% card. The 14.9% card is better than the 11.9% card until this point in time. The exact calculation of when the 11.9% card became better is complicated and not very useful, given that you are only considering a one-year time period. In general, you want to go with the deal that has the lower initial balance *only* if you plan to transfer your balance again soon.

Example 10.5:

I need to borrow $3,000. I can afford to spend $100 per month to pay back the debt. I will make $100 payments every month for one year. I have a choice between two credit cards; both have a fixed interest rate for one year. The first card has an interest rate of 19.8%, a $15 annual fee and a cash advance policy of 2% of the amount advanced, not less than $2 or greater than $20 ($2<2%<20). The second card has an interest rate of 17.9%, $50 annual fee and a cash advance fee policy of 2.5% of the amount advanced not less than $2 ($2<2.5%). Which card should I use if I want to have paid back the most money toward that debt after exactly 12 payments?

Solution 10.5:
PART 1: Solve for the Future Value of the loan if credit card 1 is used.

Step 1: Calculate all cash advance fees and annual fees.
Find 2% of $3,000.   (.02) x ($3,000) = $60
Compare to the minimum and maximum charges.
Since $60 is greater than the $20 maximum, the cash advance fee is $20.
Annual fee is $15. Therefore, total fees are:
$20 + $15 = $35
Total principal = $3,000 + $35 = $3035

Step 2: Find the Balance and Payment Factor for 19.8% in the table (page 134).
Balance Factor = 1.2170
Payment Factor = 13.1512

Step 3: Compute the Future Value of the $3,035 using the Factors.
Future Value = (Principal x Balance Factor) - (Payment x Payment Factor)
Future Value = ($3,035 x 1.2170) - ($100 x 13.1512)
Future Value = ($3,693.60) - ($1,315.12)

Future Value = $2,378.48

PART 2: Solve for the Future Value of the loan if credit card 2 is used.

Step 1: Calculate all cash advance fees and annual fees.
Find 2.5% of $3,000.   (.025) x ($3,000) = $75
Compare to the minimum and maximum charges.
Since the maximum charge is unlimited, the cash advance fee is $75.
Annual fee is $50. Therefore, total fees are:
$75 + $50 = $125
Total principal = $3,000 + $125 = $3125

Step 2: Find the Balance and Payment Factor for 17.9% in the table (page 134).
Balance Factor = 1.1944
Payment Factor = 13.0351

Step 3: Compute the Future Value of the $3,125 using the Factors.

Future Value = (Principal x Balance Factor) - (Payment x Payment Factor)

Future Value = ($3,125 x 1.1944) - ($100 x 13.0351)

Future Value = ($3,732.50) - ($1,303.51)

Future Value = $2,428.99

The 19.8% card is the better card in this example because the Future Value of the amount borrowed is less than the Future Value of the 17.9% card.   The amount saved over the course of the year is the difference between the Future Values.

Total Saved = $2,428.99 - $2,378.48 = $50.51

Even though card 2 has a 17.9% rate, 2.1% less than card 1, the fees charged are so great that the low rate card cannot create a lower balance at any time during the year.

Example 10.6:

I need to borrow $500. I can afford to spend $20 per month to pay back the debt. I will make $20 payments every month for one year. I have a choice between two credit cards and both have a fixed interest rate for one year. The first card has an interest rate of 19.8%, no annual fee or cash advance fees. The second card has an interest rate of 6.9%, $39 annual fee and a cash advance fee policy of 2% of the amount borrowed, not less than $2 or greater than $20 ($2<2%<$20). Which card should I use if I want to have paid back the most money toward that debt after exactly 12 payments?

Solution 10.6:
PART 1: Solve for the Future Value of the loan if credit card 1 is used.

Step 1: Calculate all cash advance fees and annual fees.
No annual fees or cash advance fees.
Total principal = $500

Step 2: Find the Balance and Payment Factor for 19.8% in the table (page 134).
Balance Factor = 1.2170
Payment Factor = 13.1512

Step 3: Compute the Future Value of the $500 using the Factors.

Future Value = (Principal x Balance Factor) - (Payment x Payment Factor)

Future Value = ($500 x 1.2170) - ($20 x 13.1512)

Future Value = ($608.50) - ($263.02)

Future Value = $345.48

PART 2: Solve for the Future Value of the loan if credit card 2 is used.

Step 1: Calculate all cash advance fees and annual fees.

Find 2% of $500.   (.02) x ($500) = $10

Compare to the minimum and maximum charges.

Since $10 is greater than the minimum fee and less than the maximum fee, $10 is the cash advance fee.

Annual fee is $39. Therefore, total fees are:

$10 + $39 = $49

Total principal = $500 + $49 = $549

Step 2: Find the Balance and Payment Factor for 6.9% in the table (page 133).

Balance Factor =   1.0712

Payment Factor = 12.3869

Step 3: Compute the Future Value of the $549 using the Factors.

Future Value = (Principal x Balance Factor) - (Payment x Payment Factor)

Future Value = ($549 x 1.0712) - ($20 x 12.3869)

Future Value = ($588.09) - ($247.74)

Future Value = $340.35

Total Saved = $345.48 - $340.35 = $5.13

The 6.9% card is the better card, in this example because the Future Value of the amount borrowed is less than the Future Value of the 19.8% card. This problem might seem trivial, comparing a 19.8% card to a 6.9% card. It seems obvious that because the rate is so much lower on card 2 that this would be the best card. That is the way it turned out. But you might be surprised to find that the dollar savings ($5.13) is so small when the difference between the rates is so large.

What would happen if the monthly payment in example 10.6 were greater?

Example 10.7:
Same as example 10.6, but the monthly payment is now $45.

Solution 10.7:
Step 1: Find Future Value for Credit Card 1.
      Future Value = ($500 x 1.2170) - ($45 x 13.1512)
      Future Value = ($608.50) - ($591.80)

Future Value = $16.70

Step 2: Find Future Value for Credit Card 2.
      Future Value = ($549 x 1.0712) - ($45 x 12.3869)
      Future Value = ($588.09) - ($557.41)

Future Value = $30.68

Total Saved = $30.68 - $16.70 = $13.98

Now the 19.8% card is better by $13.98!   This is because the amount advanced, $500, is relatively small and the payments are high. The money is being paid back so quickly that the interest rate has almost no effect and the main consideration is the $49 in fees that the 6.9% card is charging. This proves that you need to **do the math** to ensure that you save money.

Even though $13.98 is a small amount to save, I would rather keep it then send it to the bank. When you're constantly moving money around trying to save in interest charges, these small amounts add up quickly.

INCENTIVES

This chapter and the included examples will help you make your credit transfer decisions. There are other incentives that make one card better than another:

1. **Fixed rate for a specific time period.** This makes comparisons with other cards easier and gives you some insurance that your debt will grow at a foreseeable rate.

2. **Cash-back bonuses for balance transfers.** Some banks actually pay you to transfer balances. The deals most common are around 1% of the amount transferred with no transfer fees. This must be taken into consideration when doing your analysis. If you transfer $5,000 to one of these cards, you receive a $50 (1%) credit bringing your starting principal down to $4,950.

3. **No fee for balance transfers.**

4. **No annual fee.**

5. **Low interest rate.**

6. **High credit limit.** The more credit you have available with good terms, the more options you have to save money when borrowing.

7. **Low Minimum Monthly Payment Policy.** The lower the monthly payment, the more flexibility you have to send money to other debts that have higher rates. A low rate card with a low Monthly Payment allows you some breathing room on your Payment Schedule.

Remember to always call your credit card banks and ask for the best deal they can give. If you remain timely with your payments, you will be in a good position to ask for a fixed lower rate.

It might seem like work to figure out the best deal, but isn't it worth $50 to $100 to solve a math problem? I think it is. When you solve ten of these problems you can save between $500 and $1000. Did you ever get that much for solving ten math problems for homework when you were in school?

CHAPTER 11

PAYING THE BILLS

Remember, the most important factor in your credit worthiness is the ability to pay on time. Planning to pay bills and following through consistently, ensures that your credit history is in good standing when future lenders inspect your credit report.

Discipline, as mentioned previously, is the key. **Carefully reviewing the mail, bills, writing out checks, balancing your checkbook, completing the worksheets and analyzing your position needs to become a habit.** Like any other routine, paying your bills and planning, becomes easier the more it is practiced.

It's like a homework assignment but of much greater significance because the decisions you make and the checks that you write have an impact on your present and future financial position.

GO THROUGH YOUR MAIL EVERY DAY

Open each envelope. If it is a bill, throw out the advertisements that are not of interest and staple the statement to the return envelope. If it is a letter that needs an immediate response you will be forced to act then; otherwise put all bills and letters into the Bills-Unpaid File.

USE THE WORKSHEET INFORMATION

Every week deposit at least the amount shown in Block A of the Payment Schedule Worksheet. This guarantees funds are available on a monthly basis for paying the bills listed on the Payment Schedule.

DECIDE WHEN TO PAY THE BILLS

The best time to write checks is when the most money is in the bank. If you follow the Payment Schedule, the money will be available — most likely on a payday. You won't necessarily have to pay bills weekly, but I would recommend not letting more than two weeks go by without acting. Once you decide on the day to do this; for example, every other Friday — don't allow anything to change your plans. Sticking to your schedule will give you a proud feeling of accomplishment and peace of mind in knowing that the task is complete.

MAKE SURE WORK AREA IS CLUTTER FREE

Don't waste your time digging through piles of junk. Whether your workspace is a desk or the kitchen table, it is imperative that this area is clean when your bill paying session is scheduled. Every piece of paper you own has its place — either in a file folder or the garbage can. Put all paperwork where it belongs every day when you go through the mail. Also, make sure your office supplies are well stocked so all necessary tools are present to complete the job efficiently.

SORTING THE BILLS-UNPAID FILE

Now that you're ready to begin, the first step is to go through the Bills-Unpaid File and determine what action must be taken for each item.

Make three piles from the mail in the file. The first pile are bills that must be paid (items for which you must write checks). Sort this pile in order by DUE DATE — bills that are due earliest are on the top. You only need to pay bills that are due earlier than the next Bill-Pay Day plus a few days.

For example, if you pay the bills every two weeks starting January 1, then the next Bill-Pay Day would be January 15. Since mail takes a few days to reach its destination, I use three days as my guide. Then the checks written on January 1 reach their destination by January 5 and checks written January 15 arrive January 19. Therefore, bills paid on January 1 must cover a time period from January 5 until the day before the next Bill-Pay Days mail arrives on January 19.

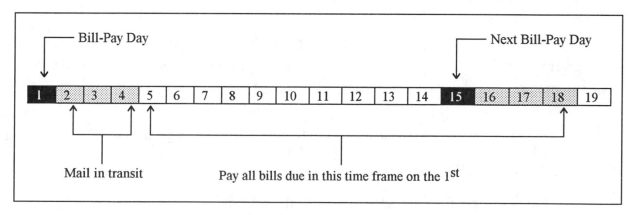

Figure 11.1: Bill-Pay Calendar.

Pile two should be composed of all bank-related statements, checks to be deposited, previous Loan Calculation Worksheet and Payment Schedule Worksheet. The worksheets are used to guide your payments and ensure that your plans are being carried out properly.

The third pile is composed of letters that need to be answered, new magazine subscriptions, medical claims, new lines of credit under consideration, and all other items that do not fit the criteria for the first two piles.

SORTED PILES SUMMARY:

1. Bills to be paid, sorted by date order.
2. Bank statements, checks, worksheets.
3. Other material that needs attention.

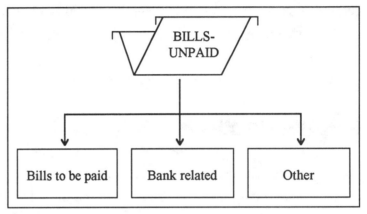

Figure 11.2: Sorting the Bills-Unpaid File.

BALANCING YOUR CHECKING ACCOUNT

Everyone knows that this should be done, but very few people actually take the time to do it. This is a vital task because the consequences of not doing it can be costly. If you don't check your records against the bank's records you might bounce future checks, and if one check bounces then all the ones that follow will also bounce. **A $25 (more or less) cost for a bounced check makes it necessary to know your checking account balance.** Furthermore, creditors do not look kindly on customers whose checks bounce.

Most banks include a worksheet located on the back of the monthly statement that will assist you in balancing your account. If your bank does not supply this sheet, you will want to use the Checking Account Balancing Worksheet in this section.

How to reconcile the checking account using the Checking Account Balancing Worksheet:

1. Enter the Statement Closing Date on line 1 of the worksheet.

2. Enter the Statement Ending Balance from your bank statement in line 2.

3. Create an entry in your checking account's transaction register for the total of all bank services charges and fees listed in your bank statement. Deduct this amount from your transaction register balance just like any other transaction.

4. Create an entry in your transaction register for interest paid. Add this amount to the balance. This completes the process of updating your register with current transactions.

5. Enter the current balance (after steps 1 through 4) of the transaction register in line 3 of the worksheet.

6. Mark all transactions in your transaction register that also appear in your bank statement — with a check mark (✓). This includes all checks, cash machine (MAC, SAM, etc.) transactions, debit card transactions, and bank service charges and fees. By keeping an accurate record of all transactions, you will be able to reference them in the future and locate canceled checks if necessary.

7. Use the Deposits Not Listed area of the worksheet to list deposits that are not included in your bank statement but do appear in your transaction register. These are the deposits that are not marked (✓). Add these up and place the total on line 4.

8. Add lines 2 and 4 to find the Subtotal for line 5.

9. Use the Withdrawals Not Listed area of the worksheet to list all checks, cash machine (MAC, SAM, etc..), and debit card transactions not included in your bank statement but do appear in your transaction register. Add these items together and enter this total in line 6.

10. Subtract line 6 from line 5 and place result in line 7. This should match the Updated Balance on your bank statement listed on line 3.

11. Staple the completed worksheet to the bank statement and file them for future reference.

BLANK CHECKING ACCOUNT BALANCING WORKSHEET

CHECKING ACCOUNT BALANCING WORKSHEET

LINE	ITEM		Amount
1	Statement Closing Date		
2	Statement Ending Balance		$
3	Updated Balance		$
	Deposits Not Listed	**Amount**	
		$	
		$	
		$	
		$	
		$	
		$	
		$	
		$	
		$	
		$	
4	Total Deposits Not Listed	$	
5	Line 2 plus line 4	$	←Subtotal
	Withdrawals Not Listed	**Amount**	
		$	
		$	
		$	
		$	
		$	
		$	
		$	
		$	
		$	
		$	
		$	
		$	
		$	
		$	
		$	
		$	
6	Total Withdrawals Not Listed	$	**Should Match**
7	**Line 5 minus line 6**	$	←**Line 3**

What to do if your account doesn't balance:

1. Check all arithmetic carefully, not only on the Checking Account Balancing Worksheet but also the Transaction Register.

2. Check to see that all numbers entered in the Withdrawals Not Listed and Deposits Not Listed worksheet sections match what's in the transaction register.

3. Make sure all deposits and withdrawals in your transaction register that occur before this reconcilement period and are not marked (✓) are accounted for in the worksheet.

4. Make sure that all cash machine and debit card transactions have been properly recorded.

5. Compare the dollar amounts listed in the transaction register, one at a time, against those same transactions listed in the bank statement.

FILE THE CANCELED CHECKS

When your bank statement arrives, canceled checks usually accompany the package. These checks should be sorted in order by check number and stored. The original box that contained the blank checks is a perfect place to store them. You should label the outside of the box: "Returned Checks No.__ through __."

PAYING THE BILLS

As you go through each bill, check all transactions listed on the credit card billing statement against the charges you made. You don't want to pay for anything you didn't buy.

When you are ready to write a check, look at the planned payments listed on the Payment Schedule Worksheet and send a check for that amount. Remember, you must abide by your payment plan even if the Minimum Payment shown on your credit card bill is lower.

Credit card representatives are usually available 24 hours a day. Don't hesitate to call your creditors concerning:

1. Getting a lower rate.
2. How long that new rate will be in effect.
3. Questionable items on your billing statement.
4. An increased line of credit.

CREATE NEW WORKSHEETS

Since many of your credit lines will be affected by new charges, you need to periodically create a new Loan Calculation Worksheet and Payment Schedule Worksheet. This doesn't have to be done every Bill-Pay Day but should definitely be completed at least once a month. Store all current worksheets by filing them in the Bills-Unpaid File.

Keep a careful watch on the policies of your cards and update the Credit Card InfoSheet. Also, add new credit offers to the Credit Offer InfoSheet.

FINALLY

The time required for the bill-paying process might be lengthy at first but gets shorter as you become more familiar with the routine. Although your work sessions might be biweekly, it may still seem as if you are constantly plagued by this chore. If you feel this way, consider: if the average bill paying session was three hours, biweekly (26 times a year), then the total time spent per year would only be 78 hours. Knowing that there are 8766 hours in a year (365¼ days), setting aside 78 of them to spend on your financial planning seems quite reasonable.

Bill-Pay Day is the time to review and analyze different credit strategies. Try to get everything related to managing your money into this day so you can enjoy the days between Bill-Pay Days without worrying about your financial problems.

CHAPTER 12

CREDIT USAGE TIPS AND HABITS

HABIT #1: Mail.

Go through the mail every day. Don't let piles of unopened envelopes build up. All important documents and bills should be placed in the Bills-Unpaid File until they are ready to be worked on when paying your bills.

TIP #1: Examine all credit offers.

Don't throw away pre-approved credit offers. File them in the Credit Offers File and record the terms on the Credit Offer InfoSheet. Always be on the lookout for new deals that can help reduce your interest rates. You never know when you may need that line of credit.

TIP #2: Elements of a good credit offer.

1. Fixed interest rate.
2. Low minimum monthly payment.
3. No annual fee.
4. Low introductory rates.
5. No fee to do balance transfers from other cards.
6. Cash back refunds.
7. Higher credit limits.
8. High cash advance limits.

HABIT #2: Payments.

Be timely with payments. The most important aspect of your credit worthiness is the ability to pay on time.

HABIT #3: Bill-Pay Day.

Pay bills at least once every two weeks.

TIP #3: Float.

"Float" normal spending by charging instead of using cash. If your card has a grace period for purchases, charge all normal spending and use the cash to pay off high interest rate debt. The grace period allows you to keep your cash for a period of time without interest charges.

TIP #4: Don't weigh down your wallet.

Carry only two credit cards. The rest should be in the Credit Card Graveyard.

HABIT #4: Clutter free.

Stay organized. Don't let clutter build up on your desk.

HABIT #5: Check your credit report periodically.

You must ensure that your credit report, or what I like to refer to as your "credit resume," is properly maintained with current and correct information. Contact these companies to receive a copy of your report:

1. **TRW**
    CBA Information Services
    PO Box 677
    Cherry Hill, NJ 08003
    (800) 682-7654

2. **Trans Union Corporation**
    Consumer Disclosure Center
    PO Box 390
    Springfield, PA 19064-0390
    (610) 690-4909

3. **Equifax**
   1600 Ptree Street NW
   Atlanta, GA 30309
   (800) 685-1111

When requesting your report you may be required to list some or all of the following information:

♦ First, middle and last name (including Jr., Sr., III).

♦ Current address.

♦ Previous addresses in the past two years, if any.

♦ Social Security Number.

♦ Date of birth.

♦ Current employer.

♦ Phone number.

♦ Signature.

♦ Applicable fee.

TIP #5: Don't cut up credit cards!

Put them in the Credit Card Graveyard." No "plastic surgery" needed. You need credit cards to reserve hotel rooms, rent cars, and buy airline tickets.

TIP #6: Good history.

Keep your credit history clean. When you have a good history of paying on time you can call to get better terms such as no annual fees or lower rates.

HABIT #6: Get it in writing.

When speaking to credit card representatives about terms and agreements, take careful notes — the person's name, time, date, and subject of conversation. Ask them to send you the agreement in writing. Also, ask representatives to make a note on their computer (on your account) mentioning the essential details of your discussion. This will avoid future confusion since you usually never get the same representative twice.

TIP #7: Overdraft protection.

Some banks allow you to have overdraft protection. If you accidentally write a check for an amount greater than your account balance the bank automatically advances money from your credit card to cover the overdraft. This way you avoid the check bouncing fee and pay the lower cash advance fee. Banks usually require that you have a credit card and/or savings account with them.

TIP #8: Don't be late.

Even if you have to cash advance money to pay a bill on time — DO IT! It is more costly to pay another 1% on a future car loan because your credit report shows late payments than to pay cash advance fees for paying on time.

HABIT #7: File it.

File all credit card receipts in the appropriate files. You need these to cross-reference purchases against credit card statements and also for possible return of merchandise.

HABIT #8: Record keeping.

Keep an accurate record of cash machine transactions. Make sure these transactions are entered in your account registers so you know the correct balance and can avoid bouncing checks.

TIP #9: Low rate vs. shorter terms.

Longer payoff terms and low-interest rates are the correct choices when financing. This gives the most flexibility because the monthly payment is lower. If you have the choice between a 5-year or 3-year car loan, with interest rates the same in both cases, chose the 5-year loan because the monthly payment is lower. You can still pay this loan back in 3 years by increasing the monthly payment but if you had a 3-year loan you are not able to reduce the payment once the loan is taken.

HABIT #9: Keep watch.

Check the interest rate on credit card statements every time you receive one! Sometimes banks "forget" how long you are entitled to a special rate or other special terms, and need a reminder.

TIP #10: Skipping payments.

Sometimes credit cards give you an option to skip a payment. If you get an option to do this on one of your low rate cards, skip that payment and use that payment for one of the higher interest rate cards. This saves the difference between the two interest rates.

TIP #11: Perks.

Don't be concerned about the various perks that credit cards offer, such as, frequent flyer miles, auto rebates, phone charges, and life insurance. The best interest rates and payment terms should be your main concern.

TIP #12: Call for better terms.

Call your credit card bank and bargain for better terms. Tell them, "I've been a good customer and if you still want my business you <u>will</u> lower my interest rate and waive the annual fee." Ask them for the best terms they have available at the moment. You will be surprised to find how quickly they accommodate your request. If your card has an annual fee ask that it be waived.

TIP #13: Beware.

Beware of credit repair companies. These businesses promise to fix your credit by correcting inaccurate information on your credit report. You can do this yourself, free of charge, as long as the information you want to change is incorrect.

TIP #14: No payoff penalties.

Never apply for a loan in which you get penalized for paying it off early. It should be stated on the loan contract if there are any penalties for early repayment.

TIP #15: Give yourself credit.

Having ten or more major credit cards is not destructive — maxing them out is. What you should do is make each bank compete for your interest payments. Even though most deals for low interest last for a short time (six months to a year), by the time one low rate runs out, another bank will be offering a similar rate for another year. The idea is to continue transferring balances to keep the APR low. If you don't have enough credit or discipline this will not be possible.

Beware - If you acquire a high amount of useable credit, this information is included in your credit report. Lenders may turn you down because you have too high a maximum. If you were applying for a mortgage, the bank might request that you close some credit accounts before they lend you money.

TIP #16: Handle the situation.

If you know you will have trouble making a payment, contact that lender and attempt a compromise. Don't avoid the payment. Be honest, sincere and take the initiative right away!

TIP #17: Transfer Balances.

Always look for ways to lower your interest rates by moving balances from one card to another. If one card has a lower purchases rate then charge your normal living expenses to that card and send the cash that you would have spent to higher interest rate debt.

TIP #18: Use the worksheets.

Follow the book and get the most from the worksheets by organizing your debt. Let the worksheets guide your decisions by pointing out the places where you need to reduce your interest rates.

HABIT #10: Do the math!

Refer to Chapters 5 and 10 when figuring out your loan problems. The trick is to word your problem like one of the examples or exercises. Analyze your situation in the same manner as the examples and then find the solution by following these examples. By doing the math you _will_ save money!

TIP #19: If denied credit get free report.

If you are denied a line of credit the lender must state the reasons why and where they got the information about your credit worthiness. The credit bureau that supplied that bank your information must send you a free copy of your credit report. Look at this situation as a time to take advantage of researching what exactly the world knows about your credit.

TIP #20: Lost or stolen.

If your credit cards are lost or stolen and you report this to the issuing bank before the card is used you have _no_ liability. If the card is used before you report it, your liability is limited to $50.

CHAPTER 13

BAD ADVICE

Here is a short list of bad advice. Some of these credit recommendations might be good in only a few limited cases but not as general rules. An explanation of my opinion follows each statement.

BAD: Pay back the credit cards with lowest balances first.

This is a good suggestion if those balances happen to have the highest interest rates. If the rate of other debt is high, it is best to pay those cards back first because charges on these accounts are more costly.

BAD: Cut up all your credit cards.

If you cut up your cards, you also cut out your options. You may need to use those credit lines to save money if rates become lower. Also, you still need to have a credit card (or cards) for emergency use.

Discipline and planning is the answer. Credit cards and loans are valuable tools in your financial life. Mastering the techniques of proper debt management eliminates the fear of having several cards. As long as they are used wisely, there is no need to cut any cards up!

BAD: Negotiating shorter terms on a loan saves more money than getting a lower rate on a longer term loan.

First, I want to show where this piece of bad advice came from. There are reasons why some people believe this. Suppose you bought a $10,000 car (everything is included in that price — bottom line) and were given a choice between a 2-year loan at 14% or a 5-year loan at 11%. The question is: which is best?

Loan 1: $10,000 at 14% for 2 years is $480.13 a month. After 2 years the total paid back is $480.13 x 24 months = $11,523.12.

Loan 2: $10,000 at 11% for 5 years is $217.42 a month. After 5 years the total paid back is $217.42 x 60 months = $13,045.45.

If you look at the total paid back on the long term loan at the lower rate (Loan 2), and compare it to the short term loan at the higher rate (Loan 1), it appears that Loan 1 is better. This is because the dollars that are being compared are at the end of each loan term. This implies that Loan 1 is better by $1,522.36 ($13,045.45-$11,523.09). **That type of comparison is not valid and is misleading!** It is not valid because the loans are being compared over two different time periods and nothing is said about the difference between the two payments over that time period.

To make the comparison fair we have to pay the same amount toward each loan over the same period of time — then true savings can be measured. Most loans allow you to make payments as large as you want to pay down the principal faster. Since the payment terms of the 2-year loan are known all that is needed for a fair comparison is the time required to pay back the 11% loan if payments are $480.13 a month. This problem is solved by following example 5.8 with the Time Remaining equal to 1 year and 11 months or 23 payments.

Loan 1: $10,000 at 14% for 2 years is $480.13 a month. After 2 years the total paid back is $480.13 x 24 months = $11,523.12.

Loan 2: $10,000 at 11% for 1 years and 11 months is $480.13 a month. After 23 payments the total paid back is $480.13 x 23 months = $11,042.99.

Now you can see the true difference between these loans and how the rate has an effect on the total paid back. Given the same principal and monthly payments, Loan 2 is better by $480.13. This makes sense because it takes 23 months to pay back Loan 2 and 24 months (2 years) to pay back Loan 1. The savings is one payment, and this is a significant amount of money.

BAD: Don't pay debt back with savings.

This advice is only good if the interest paid on your savings is greater that than the interest being charged on the debt, e.g., if your savings rate is 6% and interest charged on a loan is 5%. This is usually not the case, and as long as you don't need your savings to pay for other obligations, it is a better investment to pay back high interest debts back first.

BAD: Home equity loans are always better than credit cards because the interest is tax deductible.

This may be true in some particular cases but as a general statement it is false. There are five factors that determine if a home equity loan (second mortgage) is indeed better than a credit card or any other non-tax deductible loan:

1. Your Schedule A (from the 1040 tax returns).
2. Interest charged on the home equity loan.
3. Your tax bracket.
4. The interest on the credit card.
5. The amount of money that is borrowed.

If the dollar value of the interest charged on your home equity loan doesn't bring your Schedule A above the standard deduction then there is no benefit because you can always claim the standard deduction. If the interest charged during the year meets that condition, then the only way the home equity loan could be better is if the interest rate is less than that of the credit card.

Suppose you receive the full tax benefits of the home equity loan. Once this is true you must consider the other factors in determining which loan is better.

Home Equity Loan vs. Credit Card.

Example 13.1:

You need to borrow $10,000. You have a choice between a home equity loan with a APR of 12% and a credit card with a APR of 8.9%. If you chose the home equity loan the payments will be calculate for a 5-year payoff. This monthly payment is $222.44. You own a house and already itemize your deductions with a Schedule A in an amount that exceeds the standard deduction. You are in the 15% tax bracket. Which loan is better?

Summary of Example 13.1:

TAX BRACKET:	15%
EQUITY LOAN RATE:	12%
CREDIT CARD RATE:	8.9%
LOAN PRINCIPAL:	$10,000
LOAN TERM:	5 years

Home Equity Loan:

At the end of the first year the tax deductible interest totals $1,116.43.   After writing this off you will be refunded the full 15% of this interest or $167.46. To make the comparison useful we must take that refund into consideration by applying it to the unpaid balance of the loan, just as if it were an extra payment. When this is done, the unpaid balance becomes $8,279.69. This value represents what is still owed on the home equity loan after one year of payments and all tax considerations.

Credit Card:

Although you are able to pay a lower minimum payment to a credit card, the payment must be kept constant, in both cases, to make a fair comparison. Making the same $222.44 monthly payments on the same initial $10,000 debt leaves an unpaid balance of $8,146.32 after the first year of payments.

The unpaid balance of the credit card is $133.37 lower than the equity loan. The credit card loan has been paid off to a greater extent than the home equity loan because the interest rate is low enough (in this case) to make that true. I'm not suggesting that this is true in all cases; I am merely showing that the original advice is not true as stated. To determine which deal is better many variables must be carefully considered. Don't be fooled by the promise of tax advantages when making borrowing decisions.

Appendix 3 contains a table to assist you in comparing second mortgages to credit card rates. Using figure 13.1 you will be able to *approximate* the true APR of the second mortgage/home equity loan when tax considerations are included.

True APR for Second Mortgages

Loan APR	TAX BRACKET				
	15.00%	28.00%	31.00%	36.00%	39.60%
6.00%	5.10%	4.32%	4.14%	3.84%	3.62%
6.25%	5.31%	4.50%	4.31%	4.00%	3.78%
6.50%	5.53%	4.68%	4.49%	4.16%	3.93%
6.75%	5.74%	4.86%	4.66%	4.32%	4.08%
7.00%	5.95%	5.04%	4.83%	4.48%	4.23%
7.25%	6.16%	5.22%	5.00%	4.64%	4.38%
7.50%	6.38%	5.40%	5.18%	4.80%	4.53%
7.75%	6.59%	5.58%	5.35%	4.96%	4.68%

Figure 13.1: Partial Table from Appendix 3.

Since there are many cases where home equity loans/second mortgages are worthwhile, you need to have some way to compare the loan interest rate with that of a credit card where there are no tax benefits. **Keep in mind that second mortgages have tax benefits only if itemized deductions are greater than the standard deduction.**

To find the true APR of a home equity loan you must first know your tax bracket. You need to consult the 1040 tax guide and your previous years tax forms to find this information. Once you know your tax bracket all you need is the interest rate of the home equity loan. Follow the arrows in figure 13.1 to solve example 13.2.

Example 13.2:
What is true APR for a second mortgage if the loan rate is 7% and you are in the 28% tax bracket with your itemized deductions greater than the standard deduction?

Solution 13.2:
Look at the True APR for Second Mortgages table in Appendix 3 (page 136 or figure 13.1).

Step 1: Find the column under Tax Bracket that shows 28%.

Step 2: Follow the Tax Bracket column down to the row on the left that indicates the **Loan APR** of 7%. The number in the block, (5.04%) is the approximate true APR for the loan when taxes are considered.

True APR = 5.04%

The solution to examples 13.2 means that if you had an option to get a second mortgage (with no other fees — application, etc.) or the choice of a credit card at 5.04% there is no difference. Both loans cost the same amount of interest. If you could get a credit card rate lower than 5.04% then that would be the better choice.

BAD: Create an emergency fund even if you have debt.

If you have debt, you must pay a price to save money. This is true because the costs of borrowing are greater than the benefits of saving.

An emergency fund is a savings account created as a reserve against unexpected crises. It has been suggested that the cash value of this fund be equal to six months pay and be deposited in an account (savings) that can be readily withdrawn. This money would be used for crucial circumstances — loss of a job, medical problems, unforeseen car repairs, etc. I agree with this concept only if:

1. You have no debt that has a higher interest rate than your emergency fund savings account.
2. You have no lines of cash credit available for immediate use.

The problem with an emergency fund is that in most emergencies you can't get to the bank to withdraw the needed cash. Also, many businesses don't accept checks but take credit cards. **The biggest argument against such an account is the high interest you are paying on your debts compared to the low interest savings on the emergency fund.** If that is the case then you are actually paying a fee to create your emergency fund.

It is better is to pay the money that you would put toward the emergency fund into payments on the credit line with the highest interest rate. Because of the differences in interest rates, you reduce your loan balances faster than you can save money. As long as the credit account allows cash advances, you will be able to get that same money back if an emergency does come up.

Emergency fund example
Example 13.3:

You have three years to create money for use in an emergency. The existing debt on a credit card that is charged to the maximum limit is $2,000 with a 19.8% interest rate and a minimum payment of $61 (minimum payment is $\frac{1}{33}$ of the balance). The local bank pays 3% on a savings account which could be used for the emergency fund. After all expenses are paid each month, an extra $50 remains which can used to create an emergency fund or payoff the debt.

Summary of the basic information:

Total Debt:	$2,000
Maximum Limit:	$2,000
Minimum Payment:	$61 ($\frac{1}{33}$ of the balance)
Interest Rate:	19.8%
Savings Interest Rate:	3%
After-expense money:	$50

Therefore, the total money that is paid toward the debt and/or emergency fund is $111 ($61+$50).

Strategy 1:

Deposit $50 a month for 3 years (36 months) in the emergency fund and pay the Minimum Payments on the credit card. As the credit card balance drops, so does the Minimum Payment. As this happens, the extra money from this difference is deposited into the fund to make it grow faster.

After paying the Minimum Payment on the debt for 36 months there is still an unpaid balance of $1,212, leaving $788 in available credit. The actual emergency fund has grown significantly with a balance of $2,362. Therefore, the amount of emergency money that can be used is the amount in the emergency fund *plus* the available credit totaling $3,150.

Strategy 2:

Because the debt interest rate is greater than the rate of savings, the extra $50 every month is paid toward the debt. If the debt is ever paid off then the $111 will be saved in the emergency fund account for the remainder of the 3 years (36 months).

Another way to view this strategy is to notice that there is a total of $111 going to savings and/or debt. This total amount is applied toward the debt and if the debt is ever paid off then this total will be saved in the emergency fund account.

By paying $111 per month toward the debt it is possible to pay it off completely in only 22 months, which means the $111 can be saved in the emergency fund for the last 14 months. This leaves the entire maximum of $2,000 available on the credit card and the money saved will grow to $1,630, creating a total of $3,630 in available money.

Conclusions for example 13.3:

Notice which strategy results in more money. Strategy 2 commands $3,630 and Strategy 1 commands $3,150. Strategy 2 has accumulated $480 more in useable money. Moreover, most of the money is easily accessible through the use of that credit card, and the original debt on the card has been completely paid off. From this point forward the entire $111 can used for any purpose.

The bottom line is, as long as you have high interest rate debt you cannot have true savings. You might be able to accumulate money in an account, but you pay a fee for the privilege of having that account, and the cost of that fee is the difference between the two interest rates. The greater the difference, the greater the fee. In this previous example the fee for using Strategy 1 was $480.

Again, maintaining a good reputation with your creditors is vital for having access to needed money in an emergency. To keep that reputation means paying on time and with at least the minimum payment.

TIME-REMAINING TABLES

Time Remaining on Loans

6% to 9.5%

0 to 3 years

Years	Months	6.00%	6.50%	7.00%	7.50%	8.00%	8.50%	9.00%	9.50%
0	1	0.9950	0.9946	0.9942	0.9938	0.9934	0.9930	0.9926	0.9921
0	2	1.9851	1.9839	1.9826	1.9814	1.9802	1.9789	1.9777	1.9765
0	3	2.9702	2.9678	2.9653	2.9629	2.9604	2.9580	2.9556	2.9531
0	4	3.9505	3.9464	3.9423	3.9383	3.9342	3.9302	3.9261	3.9221
0	5	4.9259	4.9198	4.9137	4.9076	4.9015	4.8955	4.8894	4.8834
0	6	5.8964	5.8879	5.8794	5.8709	5.8625	5.8540	5.8456	5.8372
0	7	6.8621	6.8508	6.8395	6.8282	6.8170	6.8058	6.7946	6.7835
0	8	7.8230	7.8085	7.7940	7.7796	7.7652	7.7509	7.7366	7.7224
0	9	8.7791	8.7610	8.7430	8.7251	8.7072	8.6894	8.6716	8.6539
0	10	9.7304	9.7084	9.6865	9.6647	9.6429	9.6212	9.5996	9.5780
0	11	10.6770	10.6507	10.6245	10.5984	10.5724	10.5465	10.5207	10.4949
1	0	11.6189	11.5880	11.5571	11.5264	11.4958	11.4653	11.4349	11.4047
1	1	12.5562	12.5201	12.4843	12.4486	12.4130	12.3776	12.3423	12.3072
1	2	13.4887	13.4473	13.4061	13.3651	13.3242	13.2835	13.2430	13.2027
1	3	14.4166	14.3695	14.3225	14.2758	14.2293	14.1831	14.1370	14.0911
1	4	15.3399	15.2867	15.2337	15.1810	15.1285	15.0763	15.0243	14.9726
1	5	16.2586	16.1989	16.1395	16.0804	16.0217	15.9632	15.9050	15.8472
1	6	17.1728	17.1063	17.0401	16.9744	16.9089	16.8439	16.7792	16.7148
1	7	18.0824	18.0087	17.9355	17.8627	17.7903	17.7184	17.6468	17.5757
1	8	18.9874	18.9063	18.8257	18.7456	18.6659	18.5867	18.5080	18.4298
1	9	19.8880	19.7991	19.7107	19.6229	19.5357	19.4490	19.3628	19.2772
1	10	20.7841	20.6870	20.5906	20.4948	20.3997	20.3051	20.2112	20.1179
1	11	21.6757	21.5702	21.4654	21.3613	21.2579	21.1553	21.0533	20.9520
2	0	22.5629	22.4486	22.3351	22.2224	22.1105	21.9995	21.8891	21.7796
2	1	23.4456	23.3222	23.1998	23.0782	22.9575	22.8377	22.7188	22.6007
2	2	24.3240	24.1912	24.0594	23.9286	23.7988	23.6700	23.5422	23.4153
2	3	25.1980	25.0555	24.9141	24.7738	24.6346	24.4965	24.3595	24.2236
2	4	26.0677	25.9151	25.7638	25.6137	25.4648	25.3172	25.1707	25.0254
2	5	26.9330	26.7701	26.6086	26.4484	26.2896	26.1321	25.9759	25.8210
2	6	27.7941	27.6205	27.4485	27.2779	27.1088	26.9412	26.7751	26.6104
2	7	28.6508	28.4663	28.2835	28.1023	27.9227	27.7447	27.5683	27.3935
2	8	29.5033	29.3076	29.1137	28.9215	28.7312	28.5425	28.3557	28.1705
2	9	30.3515	30.1443	29.9390	29.7357	29.5343	29.3348	29.1371	28.9414
2	10	31.1955	30.9765	30.7596	30.5448	30.3320	30.1214	29.9128	29.7062
2	11	32.0354	31.8042	31.5754	31.3488	31.1246	30.9025	30.6827	30.4650
3	0	32.8710	32.6275	32.3865	32.1479	31.9118	31.6781	31.4468	31.2179

Time Remaining on Loans

6% to 9.5%
3 to 6 years

Years	Months	6.00%	6.50%	7.00%	7.50%	8.00%	8.50%	9.00%	9.50%
3	1	33.7025	33.4463	33.1928	32.9420	32.6938	32.4483	32.2053	31.9648
3	2	34.5299	34.2607	33.9945	33.7312	33.4707	33.2130	32.9581	32.7059
3	3	35.3531	35.0708	34.7916	34.5155	34.2424	33.9724	33.7053	33.4411
3	4	36.1722	35.8764	35.5840	35.2949	35.0090	34.7264	34.4469	34.1706
3	5	36.9873	36.6778	36.3718	36.0695	35.7706	35.4751	35.1831	34.8944
3	6	37.7983	37.4748	37.1551	36.8392	36.5270	36.2186	35.9137	35.6124
3	7	38.6053	38.2675	37.9338	37.6042	37.2785	36.9568	36.6389	36.3249
3	8	39.4082	39.0559	38.7080	38.3644	38.0250	37.6898	37.3587	37.0317
3	9	40.2072	39.8401	39.4777	39.1199	38.7666	38.4177	38.0732	37.7330
3	10	41.0022	40.6201	40.2430	39.8707	39.5032	39.1404	38.7823	38.4288
3	11	41.7932	41.3959	41.0038	40.6169	40.2350	39.8581	39.4862	39.1191
4	0	42.5803	42.1675	41.7602	41.3584	40.9619	40.5707	40.1848	39.8039
4	1	43.3635	42.9349	42.5122	42.0953	41.6840	41.2784	40.8782	40.4835
4	2	44.1428	43.6982	43.2599	42.8276	42.4013	41.9810	41.5664	41.1576
4	3	44.9182	44.4574	44.0032	43.5554	43.1139	42.6787	42.2496	41.8265
4	4	45.6897	45.2125	44.7422	44.2786	43.8218	43.3715	42.9276	42.4901
4	5	46.4575	45.9635	45.4769	44.9974	44.5249	44.0594	43.6006	43.1485
4	6	47.2214	46.7105	46.2074	45.7117	45.2235	44.7425	44.2686	43.8018
4	7	47.9814	47.4535	46.9336	46.4216	45.9173	45.4207	44.9316	44.4499
4	8	48.7378	48.1924	47.6556	47.1270	46.6066	46.0942	45.5897	45.0929
4	9	49.4903	48.9274	48.3734	47.8281	47.2913	46.7630	46.2429	45.7308
4	10	50.2391	49.6584	49.0871	48.5248	47.9715	47.4270	46.8912	46.3638
4	11	50.9842	50.3855	49.7966	49.2172	48.6472	48.0864	47.5347	46.9918
5	0	51.7256	51.1087	50.5020	49.9053	49.3184	48.7412	48.1734	47.6148
5	1	52.4632	51.8279	51.2033	50.5891	49.9852	49.3913	48.8073	48.2330
5	2	53.1973	52.5433	51.9006	51.2687	50.6475	50.0369	49.4365	48.8463
5	3	53.9276	53.2549	52.5938	51.9440	51.3055	50.6779	50.0611	49.4548
5	4	54.6543	53.9626	53.2829	52.6152	51.9591	51.3145	50.6810	50.0585
5	5	55.3775	54.6665	53.9681	53.2822	52.6084	51.9465	51.2963	50.6574
5	6	56.0970	55.3666	54.6493	53.9450	53.2534	52.5741	51.9070	51.2517
5	7	56.8129	56.0629	55.3266	54.6038	53.8941	53.1973	52.5131	51.8413
5	8	57.5253	56.7555	55.9999	55.2584	54.5305	53.8161	53.1147	52.4262
5	9	58.2341	57.4443	56.6694	55.9090	55.1628	54.4305	53.7119	53.0066
5	10	58.9394	58.1294	57.3349	56.5555	55.7909	55.0407	54.3046	53.5824
5	11	59.6412	58.8109	57.9966	57.1980	56.4148	55.6465	54.8929	54.1537
6	0	60.3395	59.4886	58.6544	57.8365	57.0345	56.2481	55.4768	54.7205

Time Remaining on Loans

6% to 9.5%

6 to 9 years

Years	Months	6.00%	6.50%	7.00%	7.50%	8.00%	8.50%	9.00%	9.50%
6	1	61.0343	60.1628	59.3085	58.4711	57.6502	56.8454	56.0564	55.2828
6	2	61.7257	60.8333	59.9587	59.1017	58.2618	57.4386	56.6317	55.8408
6	3	62.4136	61.5001	60.6052	59.7284	58.8693	58.0275	57.2027	56.3943
6	4	63.0982	62.1634	61.2479	60.3512	59.4728	58.6124	57.7694	56.9435
6	5	63.7793	62.8231	61.8869	60.9701	60.0723	59.1931	58.3319	57.4884
6	6	64.4570	63.4793	62.5222	61.5852	60.6679	59.7697	58.8902	58.0290
6	7	65.1313	64.1319	63.1538	62.1965	61.2595	60.3423	59.4444	58.5653
6	8	65.8023	64.7810	63.7817	62.8040	61.8472	60.9108	59.9944	59.0975
6	9	66.4700	65.4266	64.4060	63.4077	62.4310	61.4754	60.5404	59.6255
6	10	67.1343	66.0687	65.0267	64.0076	63.0109	62.0360	61.0823	60.1493
6	11	67.7953	66.7074	65.6438	64.6039	63.5870	62.5926	61.6201	60.6690
7	0	68.4530	67.3426	66.2573	65.1964	64.1593	63.1453	62.1540	61.1846
7	1	69.1075	67.9744	66.8672	65.7852	64.7277	63.6942	62.6838	61.6962
7	2	69.7587	68.6028	67.4736	66.3704	65.2925	64.2391	63.2098	62.2037
7	3	70.4067	69.2278	68.0765	66.9520	65.8534	64.7803	63.7318	62.7073
7	4	71.0514	69.8495	68.6759	67.5299	66.4107	65.3176	64.2499	63.2069
7	5	71.6930	70.4678	69.2718	68.1042	66.9643	65.8512	64.7642	63.7026
7	6	72.3313	71.0828	69.8643	68.6750	67.5142	66.3810	65.2746	64.1944
7	7	72.9665	71.6944	70.4533	69.2423	68.0604	66.9070	65.7812	64.6823
7	8	73.5985	72.3028	71.0389	69.8060	68.6031	67.4294	66.2841	65.1664
7	9	74.2273	72.9079	71.6211	70.3662	69.1421	67.9481	66.7832	65.6467
7	10	74.8531	73.5097	72.2000	70.9229	69.6776	68.4632	67.2787	66.1232
7	11	75.4757	74.1083	72.7754	71.4762	70.2096	68.9746	67.7704	66.5960
8	0	76.0952	74.7036	73.3476	72.0260	70.7380	69.4824	68.2584	67.0651
8	1	76.7117	75.2958	73.9164	72.5724	71.2629	69.9867	68.7429	67.5305
8	2	77.3250	75.8847	74.4819	73.1155	71.7843	70.4874	69.2237	67.9922
8	3	77.9354	76.4705	75.0442	73.6551	72.3023	70.9846	69.7009	68.4503
8	4	78.5426	77.0531	75.6031	74.1914	72.8169	71.4783	70.1746	68.9048
8	5	79.1469	77.6326	76.1589	74.7244	73.3280	71.9685	70.6448	69.3557
8	6	79.7482	78.2090	76.7114	75.2541	73.8358	72.4553	71.1115	69.8031
8	7	80.3464	78.7823	77.2607	75.7804	74.3402	72.9386	71.5746	70.2470
8	8	80.9417	79.3524	77.8068	76.3035	74.8412	73.4186	72.0344	70.6874
8	9	81.5341	79.9195	78.3498	76.8234	75.3390	73.8952	72.4907	71.1243
8	10	82.1234	80.4836	78.8896	77.3400	75.8334	74.3684	72.9436	71.5578
8	11	82.7099	81.0446	79.4263	77.8534	76.3246	74.8383	73.3932	71.9879
9	0	83.2934	81.6026	79.9598	78.3637	76.8125	75.3049	73.8394	72.4146

Time Remaining on Loans

10% to 13.5%
0 to 3 years

Years	Months	10.00%	10.50%	11.00%	11.50%	12.00%	12.50%	13.00%	13.50%
0	1	0.9917	0.9913	0.9909	0.9905	0.9901	0.9897	0.9893	0.9889
0	2	1.9753	1.9741	1.9728	1.9716	1.9704	1.9692	1.9680	1.9667
0	3	2.9507	2.9483	2.9458	2.9434	2.9410	2.9386	2.9362	2.9337
0	4	3.9180	3.9140	3.9100	3.9060	3.9020	3.8980	3.8940	3.8900
0	5	4.8774	4.8714	4.8654	4.8594	4.8534	4.8475	4.8415	4.8356
0	6	5.8288	5.8205	5.8121	5.8038	5.7955	5.7872	5.7789	5.7707
0	7	6.7724	6.7613	6.7502	6.7392	6.7282	6.7172	6.7063	6.6953
0	8	7.7081	7.6940	7.6798	7.6657	7.6517	7.6377	7.6237	7.6097
0	9	8.6362	8.6186	8.6010	8.5835	8.5660	8.5486	8.5313	8.5139
0	10	9.5565	9.5351	9.5138	9.4925	9.4713	9.4502	9.4291	9.4081
0	11	10.4693	10.4437	10.4183	10.3929	10.3676	10.3424	10.3173	10.2923
1	0	11.3745	11.3445	11.3146	11.2848	11.2551	11.2255	11.1960	11.1667
1	1	12.2722	12.2374	12.2027	12.1682	12.1337	12.0995	12.0653	12.0313
1	2	13.1626	13.1226	13.0828	13.0432	13.0037	12.9644	12.9253	12.8864
1	3	14.0455	14.0001	13.9549	13.9099	13.8651	13.8205	13.7761	13.7319
1	4	14.9212	14.8700	14.8190	14.7683	14.7179	14.6677	14.6177	14.5680
1	5	15.7896	15.7323	15.6753	15.6186	15.5623	15.5061	15.4503	15.3948
1	6	16.6508	16.5872	16.5239	16.4609	16.3983	16.3360	16.2740	16.2124
1	7	17.5050	17.4346	17.3647	17.2951	17.2260	17.1573	17.0889	17.0209
1	8	18.3520	18.2747	18.1979	18.1215	18.0456	17.9701	17.8950	17.8204
1	9	19.1921	19.1075	19.0235	18.9400	18.8570	18.7745	18.6925	18.6111
1	10	20.0252	19.9331	19.8416	19.7507	19.6604	19.5706	19.4815	19.3929
1	11	20.8514	20.7515	20.6523	20.5537	20.4558	20.3586	20.2620	20.1660
2	0	21.6709	21.5629	21.4556	21.3491	21.2434	21.1384	21.0341	20.9306
2	1	22.4835	22.3671	22.2516	22.1370	22.0232	21.9102	21.7980	21.6866
2	2	23.2894	23.1645	23.0404	22.9174	22.7952	22.6740	22.5536	22.4342
2	3	24.0887	23.9549	23.8221	23.6903	23.5596	23.4299	23.3012	23.1735
2	4	24.8813	24.7384	24.5966	24.4560	24.3164	24.1780	24.0408	23.9046
2	5	25.6674	25.5151	25.3641	25.2143	25.0658	24.9185	24.7724	24.6275
2	6	26.4470	26.2851	26.1246	25.9655	25.8077	25.6513	25.4962	25.3424
2	7	27.2202	27.0485	26.8782	26.7095	26.5423	26.3765	26.2122	26.0494
2	8	27.9870	27.8052	27.6250	27.4465	27.2696	27.0943	26.9206	26.7484
2	9	28.7474	28.5553	28.3650	28.1765	27.9897	27.8047	27.6214	27.4397
2	10	29.5016	29.2989	29.0983	28.8995	28.7027	28.5077	28.3146	28.1234
2	11	30.2495	30.0361	29.8249	29.6157	29.4086	29.2035	29.0004	28.7994
3	0	30.9912	30.7669	30.5449	30.3251	30.1075	29.8921	29.6789	29.4679

Time Remaining on Loans

10% to 13.5%

3 to 6 years

Years	Months	10.00%	10.50%	11.00%	11.50%	12.00%	12.50%	13.00%	13.50%
3	1	31.7268	31.4914	31.2583	31.0277	30.7995	30.5737	30.3501	30.1289
3	2	32.4564	32.2095	31.9653	31.7237	31.4847	31.2481	31.0141	30.7826
3	3	33.1799	32.9215	32.6659	32.4131	32.1630	31.9157	31.6710	31.4290
3	4	33.8974	33.6272	33.3601	33.0959	32.8347	32.5764	32.3209	32.0683
3	5	34.6090	34.3269	34.0480	33.7723	33.4997	33.2302	32.9638	32.7004
3	6	35.3147	35.0204	34.7296	34.4422	34.1581	33.8773	33.5998	33.3255
3	7	36.0146	35.7080	35.4051	35.1058	34.8100	34.5178	34.2290	33.9436
3	8	36.7087	36.3896	36.0744	35.7630	35.4555	35.1516	34.8514	34.5549
3	9	37.3970	37.0653	36.7376	36.4141	36.0945	35.7789	35.4672	35.1593
3	10	38.0797	37.7351	37.3948	37.0589	36.7272	36.3997	36.0764	35.7570
3	11	38.7567	38.3991	38.0461	37.6976	37.3537	37.0142	36.6790	36.3481
4	0	39.4282	39.0573	38.6914	38.3303	37.9740	37.6223	37.2752	36.9326
4	1	40.0940	39.7099	39.3309	38.9570	38.5881	38.2241	37.8650	37.5106
4	2	40.7544	40.3568	39.9645	39.5777	39.1961	38.8197	38.4485	38.0822
4	3	41.4093	40.9980	40.5924	40.1925	39.7981	39.4092	39.0257	38.6474
4	4	42.0589	41.6337	41.2146	40.8015	40.3942	39.9926	39.5967	39.2064
4	5	42.7030	42.2639	41.8312	41.4047	40.9844	40.5700	40.1616	39.7591
4	6	43.3418	42.8886	42.4421	42.0022	41.5687	41.1415	40.7205	40.3056
4	7	43.9754	43.5080	43.0475	42.5940	42.1472	41.7070	41.2734	40.8461
4	8	44.6037	44.1219	43.6474	43.1802	42.7200	42.2667	41.8203	41.3806
4	9	45.2268	44.7305	44.2419	43.7608	43.2871	42.8207	42.3614	41.9091
4	10	45.8447	45.3338	44.8309	44.3359	43.8486	43.3689	42.8967	42.4317
4	11	46.4576	45.9319	45.4146	44.9056	44.4046	43.9115	43.4262	42.9486
5	0	47.0654	46.5248	45.9930	45.4698	44.9550	44.4485	43.9501	43.4597
5	1	47.6681	47.1126	46.5662	46.0287	45.5000	44.9800	44.4684	43.9650
5	2	48.2659	47.6953	47.1341	46.5823	46.0396	45.5060	44.9811	44.4648
5	3	48.8588	48.2729	47.6969	47.1306	46.5739	46.0265	45.4883	44.9590
5	4	49.4467	48.8455	48.2546	47.6738	47.1029	46.5417	45.9901	45.4477
5	5	50.0298	49.4131	48.8072	48.2117	47.6266	47.0516	46.4865	45.9310
5	6	50.6081	49.9758	49.3547	48.7446	48.1452	47.5562	46.9775	46.4089
5	7	51.1815	50.5337	49.8973	49.2724	48.6586	48.0556	47.4633	46.8815
5	8	51.7503	51.0866	50.4350	49.7952	49.1669	48.5499	47.9440	47.3488
5	9	52.3143	51.6348	50.9678	50.3130	49.6702	49.0391	48.4194	47.8110
5	10	52.8737	52.1783	51.4958	50.8259	50.1685	49.5232	48.8898	48.2679
5	11	53.4285	52.7170	52.0189	51.3340	50.6619	50.0023	49.3551	48.7198
6	0	53.9787	53.2511	52.5373	51.8372	51.1504	50.4766	49.8154	49.1667

Time Remaining on Loans

10% to 13.5%
6 to 9 years

Years	Months	10.00%	10.50%	11.00%	11.50%	12.00%	12.50%	13.00%	13.50%
6	1	54.5243	53.7805	53.0510	52.3357	51.6341	50.9459	50.2708	49.6086
6	2	55.0654	54.3053	53.5601	52.8294	52.1129	51.4103	50.7213	50.0456
6	3	55.6021	54.8256	54.0645	53.3184	52.5871	51.8700	51.1670	50.4777
6	4	56.1343	55.3413	54.5643	53.8028	53.0565	52.3250	51.6079	50.9051
6	5	56.6621	55.8526	55.0596	54.2826	53.5213	52.7752	52.0441	51.3276
6	6	57.1856	56.3595	55.5504	54.7578	53.9815	53.2209	52.4756	51.7455
6	7	57.7047	56.8619	56.0367	55.2286	54.4371	53.6619	52.9025	52.1587
6	8	58.2195	57.3600	56.5186	55.6948	54.8882	54.0983	53.3248	52.5673
6	9	58.7301	57.8538	56.9962	56.1567	55.3349	54.5303	53.7426	52.9714
6	10	59.2365	58.3433	57.4694	56.6141	55.7771	54.9578	54.1559	53.3710
6	11	59.7386	58.8286	57.9383	57.0672	56.2149	55.3810	54.5648	53.7661
7	0	60.2367	59.3096	58.4029	57.5160	56.6485	55.7997	54.9693	54.1568
7	1	60.7306	59.7865	58.8633	57.9606	57.0777	56.2142	55.3695	54.5432
7	2	61.2204	60.2592	59.3196	58.4009	57.5026	56.6243	55.7654	54.9253
7	3	61.7062	60.7278	59.7717	58.8370	57.9234	57.0302	56.1570	55.3031
7	4	62.1880	61.1924	60.2196	59.2690	58.3400	57.4320	56.5444	55.6768
7	5	62.6657	61.6529	60.6636	59.6969	58.7525	57.8296	56.9277	56.0463
7	6	63.1396	62.1095	61.1034	60.1208	59.1609	58.2231	57.3069	56.4116
7	7	63.6095	62.5621	61.5393	60.5406	59.5652	58.6126	57.6820	56.7729
7	8	64.0755	63.0107	61.9713	60.9564	59.9656	58.9980	58.0531	57.1302
7	9	64.5377	63.4555	62.3993	61.3683	60.3620	59.3795	58.4202	57.4835
7	10	64.9961	63.8964	62.8234	61.7763	60.7544	59.7570	58.7834	57.8329
7	11	65.4507	64.3335	63.2437	62.1804	61.1430	60.1306	59.1427	58.1784
8	0	65.9015	64.7668	63.6601	62.5807	61.5277	60.5004	59.4981	58.5201
8	1	66.3486	65.1963	64.0728	62.9771	61.9086	60.8664	59.8497	58.8579
8	2	66.7920	65.6221	64.4817	63.3698	62.2858	61.2286	60.1976	59.1920
8	3	67.2317	66.0442	64.8869	63.7588	62.6592	61.5871	60.5417	59.5224
8	4	67.6678	66.4627	65.2884	64.1441	63.0289	61.9418	60.8822	59.8491
8	5	68.1003	66.8775	65.6863	64.5257	63.3949	62.2930	61.2190	60.1721
8	6	68.5292	67.2887	66.0806	64.9037	63.7574	62.6405	61.5522	60.4916
8	7	68.9546	67.6964	66.4712	65.2782	64.1162	62.9844	61.8818	60.8075
8	8	69.3765	68.1005	66.8584	65.6490	64.4715	63.3247	62.2079	61.1199
8	9	69.7949	68.5011	67.2420	66.0164	64.8232	63.6616	62.5304	61.4288
8	10	70.2098	68.8983	67.6221	66.3802	65.1715	63.9950	62.8496	61.7343
8	11	70.6213	69.2919	67.9988	66.7406	65.5164	64.3249	63.1653	62.0364
9	0	71.0294	69.6822	68.3720	67.0976	65.8578	64.6515	63.4776	62.3351

Time Remaining on Loans

14% to 17.5%
0 to 3 years

Years	Months	14.00%	14.50%	15.00%	15.50%	16.00%	16.50%	17.00%	17.50%
0	1	0.9885	0.9881	0.9877	0.9872	0.9868	0.9864	0.9860	0.9856
0	2	1.9655	1.9643	1.9631	1.9619	1.9607	1.9595	1.9583	1.9571
0	3	2.9313	2.9289	2.9265	2.9241	2.9217	2.9194	2.9170	2.9146
0	4	3.8860	3.8820	3.8781	3.8741	3.8701	3.8662	3.8622	3.8583
0	5	4.8297	4.8237	4.8178	4.8119	4.8061	4.8002	4.7943	4.7885
0	6	5.7624	5.7542	5.7460	5.7378	5.7297	5.7215	5.7134	5.7053
0	7	6.6844	6.6736	6.6627	6.6519	6.6411	6.6304	6.6196	6.6089
0	8	7.5958	7.5820	7.5681	7.5543	7.5406	7.5269	7.5132	7.4995
0	9	8.4967	8.4795	8.4623	8.4452	8.4282	8.4112	8.3943	8.3774
0	10	9.3872	9.3663	9.3455	9.3248	9.3041	9.2836	9.2630	9.2426
0	11	10.2674	10.2426	10.2178	10.1931	10.1686	10.1441	10.1197	10.0954
1	0	11.1375	11.1083	11.0793	11.0504	11.0216	10.9929	10.9643	10.9359
1	1	11.9975	11.9638	11.9302	11.8967	11.8634	11.8303	11.7972	11.7643
1	2	12.8476	12.8090	12.7706	12.7323	12.6942	12.6562	12.6185	12.5808
1	3	13.6879	13.6441	13.6005	13.5572	13.5140	13.4710	13.4282	13.3856
1	4	14.5185	14.4693	14.4203	14.3715	14.3230	14.2747	14.2267	14.1789
1	5	15.3396	15.2846	15.2299	15.1755	15.1214	15.0675	15.0140	14.9607
1	6	16.1511	16.0902	16.0295	15.9692	15.9093	15.8496	15.7903	15.7313
1	7	16.9533	16.8861	16.8193	16.7529	16.6868	16.6211	16.5557	16.4908
1	8	17.7463	17.6726	17.5993	17.5265	17.4541	17.3821	17.3105	17.2394
1	9	18.5301	18.4497	18.3697	18.2902	18.2112	18.1327	18.0547	17.9772
1	10	19.3049	19.2174	19.1306	19.0442	18.9585	18.8732	18.7886	18.7044
1	11	20.0707	19.9761	19.8820	19.7886	19.6959	19.6037	19.5121	19.4212
2	0	20.8277	20.7256	20.6242	20.5235	20.4235	20.3242	20.2256	20.1277
2	1	21.5760	21.4663	21.3573	21.2491	21.1417	21.0350	20.9291	20.8240
2	2	22.3157	22.1980	22.0813	21.9654	21.8503	21.7361	21.6228	21.5103
2	3	23.0468	22.9211	22.7963	22.6725	22.5497	22.4277	22.3068	22.1867
2	4	23.7695	23.6355	23.5025	23.3706	23.2398	23.1100	22.9812	22.8535
2	5	24.4838	24.3413	24.2000	24.0599	23.9208	23.7830	23.6462	23.5106
2	6	25.1900	25.0388	24.8889	24.7403	24.5929	24.4468	24.3019	24.1583
2	7	25.8879	25.7279	25.5693	25.4121	25.2562	25.1017	24.9485	24.7967
2	8	26.5779	26.4088	26.2413	26.0752	25.9107	25.7476	25.5860	25.4259
2	9	27.2598	27.0816	26.9050	26.7300	26.5566	26.3849	26.2147	26.0460
2	10	27.9339	27.7463	27.5605	27.3764	27.1940	27.0134	26.8345	26.6573
2	11	28.6003	28.4031	28.2079	28.0145	27.8231	27.6335	27.4457	27.2597
3	0	29.2589	29.0521	28.8473	28.6445	28.4438	28.2451	28.0483	27.8536

Time Remaining on Loans

14% to 17.5%
3 to 6 years

Years	Months	14.00%	14.50%	15.00%	15.50%	16.00%	16.50%	17.00%	17.50%
3	1	29.9100	29.6933	29.4788	29.2665	29.0564	28.8484	28.6426	28.4388
3	2	30.5535	30.3268	30.1025	29.8805	29.6609	29.4436	29.2285	29.0157
3	3	31.1896	30.9528	30.7185	30.4868	30.2575	30.0307	29.8062	29.5842
3	4	31.8184	31.5713	31.3269	31.0852	30.8462	30.6098	30.3759	30.1446
3	5	32.4399	32.1824	31.9278	31.6761	31.4272	31.1810	30.9376	30.6970
3	6	33.0543	32.7863	32.5213	32.2594	32.0005	31.7445	31.4915	31.2414
3	7	33.6616	33.3829	33.1075	32.8353	32.5663	32.3004	32.0376	31.7779
3	8	34.2619	33.9724	33.6864	33.4038	33.1246	32.8487	32.5761	32.3068
3	9	34.8552	34.5549	34.2582	33.9651	33.6756	33.3896	33.1071	32.8280
3	10	35.4417	35.1304	34.8229	34.5192	34.2194	33.9232	33.6307	33.3418
3	11	36.0215	35.6990	35.3806	35.0663	34.7559	34.4495	34.1469	33.8482
4	0	36.5945	36.2608	35.9315	35.6064	35.2855	34.9687	34.6560	34.3473
4	1	37.1610	36.8160	36.4755	36.1396	35.8080	35.4808	35.1579	34.8392
4	2	37.7209	37.3645	37.0129	36.6660	36.3237	35.9860	35.6528	35.3241
4	3	38.2744	37.9065	37.5436	37.1857	36.8326	36.4844	36.1408	35.8020
4	4	38.8215	38.4420	38.0677	37.6987	37.3348	36.9759	36.6220	36.2730
4	5	39.3622	38.9711	38.5854	38.2052	37.8304	37.4609	37.0965	36.7372
4	6	39.8968	39.4938	39.0967	38.7053	38.3195	37.9392	37.5643	37.1948
4	7	40.4252	40.0104	39.6017	39.1990	38.8021	38.4110	38.0256	37.6458
4	8	40.9474	40.5208	40.1004	39.6864	39.2784	38.8765	38.4805	38.0903
4	9	41.4637	41.0250	40.5930	40.1675	39.7484	39.3356	38.9290	38.5285
4	10	41.9740	41.5233	41.0795	40.6426	40.2123	39.7885	39.3712	38.9603
4	11	42.4784	42.0156	41.5600	41.1115	40.6700	40.2353	39.8073	39.3859
5	0	42.9770	42.5020	42.0346	41.5745	41.1217	40.6760	40.2373	39.8054
5	1	43.4699	42.9827	42.5033	42.0316	41.5675	41.1107	40.6612	40.2189
5	2	43.9570	43.4576	42.9662	42.4829	42.0074	41.5396	41.0793	40.6264
5	3	44.4386	43.9268	43.4234	42.9284	42.4415	41.9626	41.4915	41.0281
5	4	44.9146	44.3904	43.8750	43.3682	42.8699	42.3799	41.8979	41.4240
5	5	45.3851	44.8485	44.3210	43.8024	43.2927	42.7915	42.2987	41.8142
5	6	45.8502	45.3011	44.7615	44.2311	43.7099	43.1975	42.6939	42.1988
5	7	46.3099	45.7483	45.1965	44.6543	44.1216	43.5980	43.0835	42.5779
5	8	46.7643	46.1902	45.6262	45.0721	44.5279	43.9931	43.4677	42.9515
5	9	47.2135	46.6268	46.0505	45.4846	44.9288	44.3829	43.8466	43.3198
5	10	47.6575	47.0581	46.4697	45.8919	45.3245	44.7673	44.2201	43.6827
5	11	48.0964	47.4844	46.8836	46.2939	45.7150	45.1465	44.5885	44.0405
6	0	48.5302	47.9055	47.2925	46.6908	46.1003	45.5206	44.9516	44.3931

Time Remaining on Loans

14% to 17.5%

6 to 9 years

Years	Months	14.00%	14.50%	15.00%	15.50%	16.00%	16.50%	17.00%	17.50%
6	1	48.9590	48.3216	47.6963	47.0827	46.4805	45.8897	45.3097	44.7406
6	2	49.3828	48.7328	48.0951	47.4695	46.8558	46.2537	45.6629	45.0831
6	3	49.8018	49.1390	48.4890	47.8514	47.2261	46.6127	46.0110	45.4207
6	4	50.2160	49.5404	48.8780	48.2285	47.5916	46.9669	46.3543	45.7535
6	5	50.6253	49.9370	49.2622	48.6007	47.9522	47.3163	46.6929	46.0815
6	6	51.0300	50.3288	49.6417	48.9682	48.3081	47.6610	47.0267	46.4047
6	7	51.4300	50.7160	50.0165	49.3310	48.6593	48.0010	47.3558	46.7234
6	8	51.8253	51.0986	50.3867	49.6892	49.0059	48.3364	47.6803	47.0374
6	9	52.2162	51.4766	50.7523	50.0428	49.3479	48.6672	48.0003	47.3469
6	10	52.6025	51.8501	51.1133	50.3919	49.6854	48.9935	48.3158	47.6520
6	11	52.9843	52.2191	51.4700	50.7366	50.0185	49.3154	48.6270	47.9527
7	0	53.3618	52.5837	51.8222	51.0768	50.3472	49.6330	48.9337	48.2491
7	1	53.7349	52.9439	52.1701	51.4128	50.6716	49.9462	49.2362	48.5412
7	2	54.1036	53.2999	52.5136	51.7444	50.9917	50.2552	49.5345	48.8291
7	3	54.4682	53.6516	52.8530	52.0718	51.3076	50.5600	49.8286	49.1128
7	4	54.8285	53.9991	53.1881	52.3950	51.6194	50.8607	50.1186	49.3925
7	5	55.1847	54.3425	53.5191	52.7141	51.9270	51.1573	50.4045	49.6682
7	6	55.5368	54.6818	53.8461	53.0292	52.2306	51.4498	50.6864	49.9399
7	7	55.8848	55.0170	54.1689	53.3402	52.5302	51.7384	50.9644	50.2077
7	8	56.2288	55.3482	54.4879	53.6473	52.8258	52.0231	51.2386	50.4717
7	9	56.5688	55.6754	54.8028	53.9504	53.1176	52.3039	51.5088	50.7318
7	10	56.9049	55.9988	55.1139	54.2497	53.4055	52.5810	51.7754	50.9883
7	11	57.2371	56.3183	55.4211	54.5451	53.6897	52.8542	52.0382	51.2410
8	0	57.5655	56.6339	55.7246	54.8368	53.9701	53.1238	52.2973	51.4901
8	1	57.8902	56.9458	56.0243	55.1248	54.2468	53.3896	52.5528	51.7356
8	2	58.2110	57.2540	56.3203	55.4091	54.5199	53.6519	52.8047	51.9776
8	3	58.5282	57.5585	56.6126	55.6898	54.7893	53.9107	53.0531	52.2161
8	4	58.8417	57.8594	56.9013	55.9669	55.0553	54.1659	53.2981	52.4512
8	5	59.1516	58.1567	57.1865	56.2404	55.3177	54.4176	53.5396	52.6829
8	6	59.4579	58.4504	57.4682	56.5105	55.5767	54.6660	53.7777	52.9113
8	7	59.7607	58.7406	57.7463	56.7771	55.8322	54.9110	54.0126	53.1364
8	8	60.0600	59.0274	58.0211	57.0404	56.0844	55.1526	54.2441	53.3583
8	9	60.3559	59.3107	58.2924	57.3002	56.3333	55.3910	54.4724	53.5769
8	10	60.6483	59.5906	58.5604	57.5568	56.5789	55.6261	54.6975	53.7924
8	11	60.9374	59.8672	58.8251	57.8101	56.8213	55.8581	54.9195	54.0049
9	0	61.2231	60.1405	59.0865	58.0601	57.0605	56.0869	55.1384	54.2143

Time Remaining on Loans

18% to 21.5%
0 to 3 years

Years	Months	18.00%	18.50%	19.00%	19.50%	20.00%	20.50%	21.00%	21.50%
0	1	0.9852	0.9848	0.9844	0.9840	0.9836	0.9832	0.9828	0.9824
0	2	1.9559	1.9547	1.9535	1.9523	1.9511	1.9499	1.9487	1.9475
0	3	2.9122	2.9098	2.9074	2.9051	2.9027	2.9003	2.8980	2.8956
0	4	3.8544	3.8505	3.8465	3.8426	3.8387	3.8348	3.8309	3.8271
0	5	4.7826	4.7768	4.7710	4.7652	4.7594	4.7536	4.7479	4.7421
0	6	5.6972	5.6891	5.6811	5.6730	5.6650	5.6570	5.6490	5.6410
0	7	6.5982	6.5876	6.5769	6.5663	6.5557	6.5452	6.5346	6.5241
0	8	7.4859	7.4724	7.4588	7.4453	7.4319	7.4184	7.4051	7.3917
0	9	8.3605	8.3437	8.3270	8.3103	8.2936	8.2770	8.2605	8.2440
0	10	9.2222	9.2019	9.1816	9.1614	9.1413	9.1212	9.1012	9.0813
0	11	10.0711	10.0470	10.0229	9.9989	9.9750	9.9512	9.9275	9.9038
1	0	10.9075	10.8792	10.8511	10.8231	10.7951	10.7673	10.7395	10.7119
1	1	11.7315	11.6989	11.6664	11.6340	11.6018	11.5696	11.5376	11.5058
1	2	12.5434	12.5061	12.4690	12.4320	12.3952	12.3585	12.3220	12.2857
1	3	13.3432	13.3010	13.2590	13.2172	13.1756	13.1341	13.0929	13.0518
1	4	14.1313	14.0839	14.0368	13.9899	13.9432	13.8967	13.8505	13.8045
1	5	14.9076	14.8549	14.8024	14.7502	14.6982	14.6465	14.5951	14.5439
1	6	15.6726	15.6142	15.5561	15.4983	15.4409	15.3837	15.3269	15.2703
1	7	16.4262	16.3619	16.2980	16.2345	16.1713	16.1085	16.0461	15.9839
1	8	17.1686	17.0983	17.0284	16.9589	16.8898	16.8212	16.7529	16.6850
1	9	17.9001	17.8235	17.7474	17.6718	17.5966	17.5218	17.4475	17.3737
1	10	18.6208	18.5378	18.4552	18.3732	18.2917	18.2107	18.1303	18.0503
1	11	19.3309	19.2411	19.1520	19.0634	18.9755	18.8881	18.8012	18.7150
2	0	20.0304	19.9338	19.8379	19.7426	19.6480	19.5540	19.4607	19.3680
2	1	20.7196	20.6160	20.5131	20.4109	20.3095	20.2088	20.1088	20.0095
2	2	21.3986	21.2878	21.1778	21.0686	20.9602	20.8525	20.7457	20.6397
2	3	22.0676	21.9494	21.8321	21.7157	21.6002	21.4855	21.3717	21.2588
2	4	22.7267	22.6010	22.4762	22.3525	22.2297	22.1078	21.9870	21.8670
2	5	23.3761	23.2427	23.1103	22.9790	22.8488	22.7197	22.5916	22.4645
2	6	24.0158	23.8746	23.7345	23.5956	23.4579	23.3213	23.1858	23.0515
2	7	24.6461	24.4969	24.3490	24.2023	24.0569	23.9128	23.7699	23.6282
2	8	25.2671	25.1098	24.9539	24.7993	24.6462	24.4943	24.3439	24.1947
2	9	25.8790	25.7134	25.5494	25.3868	25.2257	25.0661	24.9080	24.7512
2	10	26.4817	26.3078	26.1355	25.9649	25.7958	25.6283	25.4624	25.2980
2	11	27.0756	26.8932	26.7126	26.5337	26.3565	26.1811	26.0073	25.8351
3	0	27.6607	27.4697	27.2806	27.0934	26.9081	26.7245	26.5428	26.3628

Time Remaining on Loans

18% to 21.5%
3 to 6 years

Years	Months	18.00%	18.50%	19.00%	19.50%	20.00%	20.50%	21.00%	21.50%
3	1	28.2371	28.0375	27.8399	27.6442	27.4506	27.2588	27.0690	26.8812
3	2	28.8051	28.5966	28.3903	28.1862	27.9842	27.7842	27.5863	27.3904
3	3	29.3646	29.1473	28.9322	28.7195	28.5090	28.3007	28.0946	27.8907
3	4	29.9158	29.6895	29.4657	29.2443	29.0252	28.8086	28.5942	28.3822
3	5	30.4590	30.2236	29.9908	29.7607	29.5330	29.3079	29.0852	28.8650
3	6	30.9941	30.7495	30.5078	30.2688	30.0325	29.7988	29.5678	29.3394
3	7	31.5212	31.2675	31.0167	30.7688	30.5238	30.2815	30.0421	29.8053
3	8	32.0406	31.7776	31.5177	31.2608	31.0070	30.7561	30.5082	30.2631
3	9	32.5523	32.2800	32.0108	31.7450	31.4823	31.2227	30.9663	30.7129
3	10	33.0565	32.7747	32.4963	32.2214	31.9498	31.6815	31.4165	31.1547
3	11	33.5532	33.2619	32.9742	32.6902	32.4096	32.1326	31.8589	31.5887
4	0	34.0426	33.7417	33.4447	33.1514	32.8619	32.5761	32.2938	32.0151
4	1	34.5247	34.2142	33.9078	33.6054	33.3068	33.0121	32.7212	32.4340
4	2	34.9997	34.6796	34.3637	34.0520	33.7444	33.4408	33.1412	32.8455
4	3	35.4677	35.1379	34.8125	34.4915	34.1748	33.8623	33.5540	33.2498
4	4	35.9287	35.5892	35.2543	34.9240	34.5982	34.2768	33.9597	33.6469
4	5	36.3830	36.0337	35.6892	35.3496	35.0146	34.6843	34.3584	34.0371
4	6	36.8305	36.4714	36.1174	35.7683	35.4242	35.0849	34.7503	34.4204
4	7	37.2715	36.9025	36.5389	36.1804	35.8271	35.4788	35.1354	34.7970
4	8	37.7059	37.3271	36.9538	36.5859	36.2234	35.8661	35.5140	35.1669
4	9	38.1339	37.7451	37.3622	36.9849	36.6131	36.2469	35.8859	35.5303
4	10	38.5555	38.1569	37.7643	37.3775	36.9965	36.6212	36.2515	35.8873
4	11	38.9710	38.5624	38.1601	37.7638	37.3736	36.9893	36.6109	36.2381
5	0	39.3803	38.9617	38.5497	38.1440	37.7446	37.3513	36.9640	36.5826
5	1	39.7835	39.3550	38.9332	38.5181	38.1094	37.7071	37.3110	36.9211
5	2	40.1808	39.7423	39.3108	38.8862	38.4683	38.0570	37.6521	37.2537
5	3	40.5722	40.1237	39.6825	39.2484	38.8212	38.4009	37.9874	37.5803
5	4	40.9579	40.4994	40.0484	39.6048	39.1684	38.7391	38.3168	37.9013
5	5	41.3378	40.8693	40.4086	39.9555	39.5099	39.0717	38.6406	38.2166
5	6	41.7121	41.2336	40.7632	40.3006	39.8458	39.3986	38.9588	38.5263
5	7	42.0809	41.5924	41.1122	40.6402	40.1762	39.7201	39.2716	38.8306
5	8	42.4442	41.9457	41.4559	40.9744	40.5012	40.0361	39.5789	39.1295
5	9	42.8022	42.2937	41.7941	41.3032	40.8209	40.3469	39.8810	39.4232
5	10	43.1549	42.6364	42.1271	41.6268	41.1353	40.6524	40.1779	39.7117
5	11	43.5023	42.9739	42.4549	41.9452	41.4445	40.9528	40.4697	39.9951
6	0	43.8447	43.3063	42.7776	42.2585	41.7487	41.2481	40.7564	40.2735

Time Remaining on Loans

18% to 21.5%
6 to 9 years

Years	Months	18.00%	18.50%	19.00%	19.50%	20.00%	20.50%	21.00%	21.50%
6	1	44.1819	43.6336	43.0953	42.5668	42.0479	41.5385	41.0383	40.5471
6	2	44.5142	43.9559	43.4080	42.8701	42.3422	41.8240	41.3153	40.8158
6	3	44.8416	44.2734	43.7158	43.1686	42.6317	42.1047	41.5875	41.0798
6	4	45.1641	44.5860	44.0188	43.4624	42.9164	42.3807	41.8550	41.3391
6	5	45.4819	44.8939	44.3171	43.7514	43.1965	42.6521	42.1180	41.5939
6	6	45.7950	45.1971	44.6108	44.0358	43.4719	42.9189	42.3764	41.8442
6	7	46.1034	45.4957	44.8999	44.3157	43.7429	43.1812	42.6303	42.0901
6	8	46.4073	45.7898	45.1845	44.5911	44.0094	43.4391	42.8799	42.3316
6	9	46.7067	46.0794	45.4646	44.8621	44.2716	43.6927	43.1252	42.5689
6	10	47.0017	46.3646	45.7404	45.1288	44.5294	43.9420	43.3663	42.8021
6	11	47.2923	46.6455	46.0119	45.3911	44.7830	44.1872	43.6033	43.0311
7	0	47.5786	46.9221	46.2791	45.6493	45.0325	44.4282	43.8361	43.2561
7	1	47.8607	47.1945	46.5422	45.9034	45.2778	44.6651	44.0650	43.4771
7	2	48.1386	47.4628	46.8012	46.1534	45.5192	44.8981	44.2899	43.6943
7	3	48.4125	47.7270	47.0561	46.3994	45.7566	45.1272	44.5110	43.9076
7	4	48.6822	47.9872	47.3071	46.6415	45.9901	45.3524	44.7282	44.1172
7	5	48.9480	48.2435	47.5542	46.8797	46.2197	45.5739	44.9418	44.3230
7	6	49.2099	48.4958	47.7974	47.1141	46.4457	45.7916	45.1516	44.5253
7	7	49.4678	48.7443	48.0368	47.3448	46.6679	46.0057	45.3578	44.7240
7	8	49.7220	48.9891	48.2725	47.5717	46.8864	46.2162	45.5605	44.9192
7	9	49.9724	49.2301	48.5045	47.7950	47.1014	46.4231	45.7597	45.1109
7	10	50.2191	49.4675	48.7329	48.0148	47.3128	46.6266	45.9555	45.2993
7	11	50.4622	49.7013	48.9577	48.2311	47.5208	46.8266	46.1479	45.4844
8	0	50.7017	49.9315	49.1790	48.4438	47.7254	47.0233	46.3370	45.6662
8	1	50.9376	50.1582	49.3969	48.6532	47.9266	47.2167	46.5229	45.8448
8	2	51.1701	50.3815	49.6114	48.8593	48.1246	47.4068	46.7055	46.0203
8	3	51.3991	50.6014	49.8226	49.0620	48.3192	47.5937	46.8850	46.1927
8	4	51.6247	50.8180	50.0304	49.2615	48.5107	47.7775	47.0615	46.3620
8	5	51.8470	51.0312	50.2350	49.4578	48.6991	47.9583	47.2349	46.5284
8	6	52.0660	51.2413	50.4364	49.6510	48.8843	48.1359	47.4053	46.6918
8	7	52.2818	51.4481	50.6347	49.8411	49.0666	48.3106	47.5727	46.8524
8	8	52.4944	51.6518	50.8299	50.0281	49.2458	48.4824	47.7373	47.0101
8	9	52.7038	51.8524	51.0221	50.2122	49.4221	48.6513	47.8991	47.1651
8	10	52.9102	52.0500	51.2112	50.3933	49.5955	48.8173	48.0581	47.3173
8	11	53.1135	52.2445	51.3974	50.5715	49.7661	48.9805	48.2143	47.4669
9	0	53.3137	52.4361	51.5807	50.7468	49.9338	49.1411	48.3679	47.6138

Time Remaining on Loans

22% to 25.5%
0 to 3 years

Years	Months	22.00%	22.50%	23.00%	23.50%	24.00%	24.50%	25.00%	25.50%
0	1	0.9820	0.9816	0.9812	0.9808	0.9804	0.9800	0.9796	0.9792
0	2	1.9463	1.9451	1.9439	1.9427	1.9416	1.9404	1.9392	1.9380
0	3	2.8933	2.8909	2.8886	2.8862	2.8839	2.8815	2.8792	2.8769
0	4	3.8232	3.8193	3.8154	3.8116	3.8077	3.8039	3.8000	3.7962
0	5	4.7363	4.7306	4.7249	4.7192	4.7135	4.7078	4.7021	4.6964
0	6	5.6331	5.6251	5.6172	5.6093	5.6014	5.5936	5.5857	5.5779
0	7	6.5137	6.5032	6.4928	6.4824	6.4720	6.4616	6.4513	6.4410
0	8	7.3784	7.3651	7.3519	7.3387	7.3255	7.3123	7.2992	7.2862
0	9	8.2275	8.2111	8.1948	8.1785	8.1622	8.1460	8.1299	8.1138
0	10	9.0614	9.0416	9.0219	9.0022	8.9826	8.9630	8.9435	8.9241
0	11	9.8803	9.8568	9.8334	9.8101	9.7868	9.7637	9.7406	9.7176
1	0	10.6844	10.6570	10.6297	10.6025	10.5753	10.5483	10.5214	10.4946
1	1	11.4740	11.4424	11.4110	11.3796	11.3484	11.3173	11.2863	11.2554
1	2	12.2495	12.2134	12.1776	12.1418	12.1062	12.0708	12.0355	12.0004
1	3	13.0109	12.9702	12.9297	12.8894	12.8493	12.8093	12.7695	12.7299
1	4	13.7587	13.7131	13.6678	13.6226	13.5777	13.5330	13.4885	13.4442
1	5	14.4930	14.4423	14.3919	14.3418	14.2919	14.2422	14.1928	14.1437
1	6	15.2141	15.1581	15.1025	15.0471	14.9920	14.9373	14.8828	14.8286
1	7	15.9222	15.8607	15.7996	15.7389	15.6785	15.6184	15.5586	15.4992
1	8	16.6175	16.5504	16.4837	16.4174	16.3514	16.2859	16.2207	16.1559
1	9	17.3003	17.2274	17.1549	17.0828	17.0112	16.9400	16.8693	16.7989
1	10	17.9709	17.8919	17.8135	17.7355	17.6580	17.5811	17.5046	17.4286
1	11	18.6293	18.5442	18.4597	18.3757	18.2922	18.2093	18.1269	18.0451
2	0	19.2759	19.1845	19.0937	19.0035	18.9139	18.8250	18.7366	18.6488
2	1	19.9109	19.8130	19.7158	19.6193	19.5235	19.4283	19.3338	19.2400
2	2	20.5344	20.4299	20.3262	20.2233	20.1210	20.0196	19.9188	19.8188
2	3	21.1467	21.0355	20.9252	20.8156	20.7069	20.5990	20.4919	20.3856
2	4	21.7480	21.6300	21.5128	21.3966	21.2813	21.1668	21.0533	20.9406
2	5	22.3385	22.2135	22.0894	21.9664	21.8444	21.7233	21.6032	21.4841
2	6	22.9183	22.7862	22.6552	22.5253	22.3965	22.2687	22.1419	22.0162
2	7	23.4877	23.3484	23.2104	23.0734	22.9377	22.8031	22.6697	22.5373
2	8	24.0469	23.9003	23.7551	23.6111	23.4683	23.3269	23.1866	23.0476
2	9	24.5959	24.4420	24.2895	24.1384	23.9886	23.8401	23.6930	23.5472
2	10	25.1351	24.9738	24.8139	24.6555	24.4986	24.3431	24.1891	24.0364
2	11	25.6646	25.4957	25.3284	25.1627	24.9986	24.8360	24.6750	24.5155
3	0	26.1846	26.0081	25.8333	25.6602	25.4888	25.3191	25.1510	24.9845

Time Remaining on Loans

22% to 25.5%
3 to 6 years

Years	Months	22.00%	22.50%	23.00%	23.50%	24.00%	24.50%	25.00%	25.50%
3	1	26.6951	26.5110	26.3287	26.1482	25.9695	25.7925	25.6173	25.4439
3	2	27.1965	27.0047	26.8147	26.6267	26.4406	26.2564	26.0741	25.8936
3	3	27.6889	27.4892	27.2916	27.0961	26.9026	26.7111	26.5216	26.3340
3	4	28.1724	27.9649	27.7596	27.5564	27.3555	27.1566	26.9599	26.7653
3	5	28.6472	28.4318	28.2187	28.0080	27.7995	27.5933	27.3893	27.1875
3	6	29.1135	28.8901	28.6692	28.4508	28.2348	28.0212	27.8099	27.6010
3	7	29.5713	29.3400	29.1113	28.8851	28.6616	28.4405	28.2220	28.0059
3	8	30.0209	29.7816	29.5450	29.3111	29.0800	28.8515	28.6256	28.4023
3	9	30.4625	30.2150	29.9705	29.7289	29.4902	29.2542	29.0210	28.7905
3	10	30.8960	30.6405	30.3881	30.1387	29.8923	29.6489	29.4083	29.1707
3	11	31.3218	31.0582	30.7978	30.5406	30.2866	30.0356	29.7877	29.5429
4	0	31.7399	31.4682	31.1998	30.9348	30.6731	30.4147	30.1594	29.9073
4	1	32.1505	31.8706	31.5943	31.3214	31.0521	30.7861	30.5235	30.2642
4	2	32.5537	32.2656	31.9813	31.7006	31.4236	31.1501	30.8802	30.6137
4	3	32.9496	32.6534	32.3610	32.0725	31.7878	31.5069	31.2296	30.9559
4	4	33.3384	33.0340	32.7336	32.4373	32.1449	31.8565	31.5718	31.2909
4	5	33.7202	33.4076	33.0992	32.7951	32.4950	32.1991	31.9071	31.6190
4	6	34.0951	33.7743	33.4580	33.1460	32.8383	32.5348	32.2355	31.9403
4	7	34.4633	34.1343	33.8099	33.4901	33.1748	32.8639	32.5572	32.2549
4	8	34.8248	34.4876	34.1553	33.8277	33.5047	33.1863	32.8724	32.5629
4	9	35.1799	34.8345	34.4942	34.1587	33.8281	33.5023	33.1811	32.8646
4	10	35.5285	35.1750	34.8266	34.4834	34.1452	33.8120	33.4836	33.1599
4	11	35.8709	35.5092	35.1529	34.8019	34.4561	34.1154	33.7798	33.4491
5	0	36.2071	35.8372	35.4730	35.1142	34.7609	34.4128	34.0700	33.7323
5	1	36.5372	36.1592	35.7871	35.4206	35.0597	34.7043	34.3543	34.0096
5	2	36.8614	36.4753	36.0952	35.7210	35.3526	34.9899	34.6328	34.2811
5	3	37.1798	36.7856	36.3976	36.0157	35.6398	35.2698	34.9056	34.5470
5	4	37.4924	37.0902	36.6943	36.3048	35.9214	35.5441	35.1728	34.8073
5	5	37.7995	37.3891	36.9854	36.5882	36.1975	35.8130	35.4346	35.0623
5	6	38.1009	37.6826	37.2711	36.8663	36.4681	36.0764	35.6910	35.3119
5	7	38.3970	37.9706	37.5513	37.1390	36.7334	36.3346	35.9422	35.5563
5	8	38.6877	38.2534	37.8263	37.4064	36.9936	36.5876	36.1883	35.7957
5	9	38.9732	38.5309	38.0961	37.6688	37.2486	36.8355	36.4294	36.0300
5	10	39.2536	38.8033	38.3609	37.9260	37.4986	37.0785	36.6655	36.2595
5	11	39.5289	39.0708	38.6207	38.1784	37.7437	37.3166	36.8968	36.4842
6	0	39.7992	39.3333	38.8755	38.4259	37.9841	37.5500	37.1234	36.7043

Time Remaining on Loans

22% to 25.5%
6 to 9 years

Years	Months	22.00%	22.50%	23.00%	23.50%	24.00%	24.50%	25.00%	25.50%
6	1	40.0647	39.5909	39.1256	38.6686	38.2197	37.7787	37.3454	36.9197
6	2	40.3254	39.8439	39.3710	38.9067	38.4507	38.0028	37.5628	37.1307
6	3	40.5814	40.0921	39.6118	39.1402	38.6771	38.2224	37.7758	37.3373
6	4	40.8328	40.3358	39.8480	39.3692	38.8991	38.4376	37.9845	37.5396
6	5	41.0797	40.5751	40.0799	39.5938	39.1168	38.6485	38.1889	37.7376
6	6	41.3221	40.8099	40.3073	39.8141	39.3302	38.8553	38.3891	37.9316
6	7	41.5602	41.0404	40.5305	40.0302	39.5394	39.0578	38.5853	38.1215
6	8	41.7939	41.2666	40.7494	40.2421	39.7445	39.2563	38.7774	38.3075
6	9	42.0235	41.4887	40.9643	40.4500	39.9456	39.4509	38.9656	38.4896
6	10	42.2489	41.7067	41.1751	40.6539	40.1427	39.6415	39.1500	38.6679
6	11	42.4703	41.9207	41.3819	40.8538	40.3360	39.8284	39.3306	38.8425
7	0	42.6877	42.1307	41.5849	41.0499	40.5255	40.0115	39.5075	39.0134
7	1	42.9012	42.3369	41.7840	41.2422	40.7113	40.1909	39.6808	39.1808
7	2	43.1108	42.5393	41.9794	41.4309	40.8934	40.3668	39.8506	39.3448
7	3	43.3167	42.7380	42.1711	41.6159	41.0720	40.5391	40.0169	39.5053
7	4	43.5188	42.9330	42.3593	41.7974	41.2470	40.7080	40.1798	39.6624
7	5	43.7174	43.1244	42.5438	41.9754	41.4187	40.8735	40.3394	39.8164
7	6	43.9123	43.3123	42.7249	42.1499	41.5869	41.0356	40.4958	39.9671
7	7	44.1037	43.4967	42.9026	42.3211	41.7519	41.1946	40.6489	40.1146
7	8	44.2917	43.6778	43.0770	42.4891	41.9136	41.3504	40.7990	40.2591
7	9	44.4763	43.8555	43.2481	42.6538	42.0722	41.5030	40.9459	40.4006
7	10	44.6576	44.0299	43.4159	42.8153	42.2276	41.6526	41.0899	40.5391
7	11	44.8356	44.2011	43.5806	42.9737	42.3800	41.7992	41.2309	40.6748
8	0	45.0104	44.3692	43.7423	43.1291	42.5294	41.9429	41.3690	40.8076
8	1	45.1821	44.5342	43.9008	43.2815	42.6759	42.0837	41.5044	40.9377
8	2	45.3507	44.6962	44.0564	43.4310	42.8195	42.2216	41.6369	41.0651
8	3	45.5162	44.8551	44.2091	43.5776	42.9603	42.3568	41.7668	41.1898
8	4	45.6787	45.0112	44.3589	43.7214	43.0984	42.4894	41.8940	41.3119
8	5	45.8384	45.1643	44.5058	43.8624	43.2337	42.6192	42.0186	41.4315
8	6	45.9951	45.3147	44.6500	44.0007	43.3664	42.7465	42.1407	41.5486
8	7	46.1491	45.4623	44.7915	44.1364	43.4964	42.8712	42.2603	41.6632
8	8	46.3002	45.6071	44.9304	44.2695	43.6239	42.9934	42.3774	41.7755
8	9	46.4487	45.7493	45.0666	44.4000	43.7490	43.1132	42.4921	41.8855
8	10	46.5944	45.8889	45.2002	44.5279	43.8715	43.2305	42.6045	41.9931
8	11	46.7376	46.0259	45.3314	44.6535	43.9917	43.3456	42.7147	42.0985
9	0	46.8781	46.1604	45.4601	44.7766	44.1095	43.4583	42.8225	42.2017

BALANCE & PAYMENT FACTORS

Balance & Payment Factors

1 year (12 payments)

Rate	Balance Factor	Payment Factor	Rate	Balance Factor	Payment Factor	Rate	Balance Factor	Payment Factor
4.00	1.0407	12.2225	7.60	1.0787	12.4270	11.20	1.1179	12.6356
4.10	1.0418	12.2281	7.70	1.0798	12.4327	11.30	1.1190	12.6414
4.20	1.0428	12.2337	7.80	1.0808	12.4384	11.40	1.1201	12.6473
4.30	1.0439	12.2393	7.90	1.0819	12.4442	11.50	1.1213	12.6531
4.40	1.0449	12.2450	8.00	1.0830	12.4499	11.60	1.1224	12.6590
4.50	1.0459	12.2506	8.10	1.0841	12.4557	11.70	1.1235	12.6649
4.60	1.0470	12.2563	8.20	1.0852	12.4614	11.80	1.1246	12.6708
4.70	1.0480	12.2619	8.30	1.0862	12.4672	11.90	1.1257	12.6766
4.80	1.0491	12.2676	8.40	1.0873	12.4730	12.00	1.1268	12.6825
4.90	1.0501	12.2732	8.50	1.0884	12.4787	12.10	1.1279	12.6884
5.00	1.0512	12.2789	8.60	1.0895	12.4845	12.20	1.1291	12.6943
5.10	1.0522	12.2845	8.70	1.0906	12.4903	12.30	1.1302	12.7002
5.20	1.0533	12.2902	8.80	1.0916	12.4960	12.40	1.1313	12.7060
5.30	1.0543	12.2958	8.90	1.0927	12.5018	12.50	1.1324	12.7119
5.40	1.0554	12.3015	9.00	1.0938	12.5076	12.60	1.1335	12.7178
5.50	1.0564	12.3072	9.10	1.0949	12.5134	12.70	1.1347	12.7237
5.60	1.0575	12.3128	9.20	1.0960	12.5192	12.80	1.1358	12.7296
5.70	1.0585	12.3185	9.30	1.0971	12.5249	12.90	1.1369	12.7355
5.80	1.0596	12.3242	9.40	1.0982	12.5307	13.00	1.1380	12.7415
5.90	1.0606	12.3299	9.50	1.0992	12.5365	13.10	1.1392	12.7474
6.00	1.0617	12.3356	9.60	1.1003	12.5423	13.20	1.1403	12.7533
6.10	1.0627	12.3413	9.70	1.1014	12.5481	13.30	1.1414	12.7592
6.20	1.0638	12.3469	9.80	1.1025	12.5539	13.40	1.1425	12.7651
6.30	1.0649	12.3526	9.90	1.1036	12.5598	13.50	1.1437	12.7711
6.40	1.0659	12.3583	10.00	1.1047	12.5656	13.60	1.1448	12.7770
6.50	1.0670	12.3640	10.10	1.1058	12.5714	13.70	1.1459	12.7829
6.60	1.0680	12.3697	10.20	1.1069	12.5772	13.80	1.1471	12.7889
6.70	1.0691	12.3754	10.30	1.1080	12.5830	13.90	1.1482	12.7948
6.80	1.0702	12.3812	10.40	1.1091	12.5889	14.00	1.1493	12.8007
6.90	1.0712	12.3869	10.50	1.1102	12.5947	14.10	1.1505	12.8067
7.00	1.0723	12.3926	10.60	1.1113	12.6005	14.20	1.1516	12.8126
7.10	1.0734	12.3983	10.70	1.1124	12.6063	14.30	1.1528	12.8186
7.20	1.0744	12.4040	10.80	1.1135	12.6122	14.40	1.1539	12.8246
7.30	1.0755	12.4098	10.90	1.1146	12.6180	14.50	1.1550	12.8305
7.40	1.0766	12.4155	11.00	1.1157	12.6239	14.60	1.1562	12.8365
7.50	1.0776	12.4212	11.10	1.1168	12.6297	14.70	1.1573	12.8424

Balance & Payment Factors

1 year (12 payments)

Rate	Balance Factor	Payment Factor	Rate	Balance Factor	Payment Factor	Rate	Balance Factor	Payment Factor
14.80	1.1585	12.8484	18.40	1.2003	13.0656	22.00	1.2436	13.2871
14.90	1.1596	12.8544	18.50	1.2015	13.0716	22.10	1.2448	13.2933
15.00	1.1608	12.8604	18.60	1.2027	13.0777	22.20	1.2460	13.2995
15.10	1.1619	12.8663	18.70	1.2039	13.0838	22.30	1.2473	13.3057
15.20	1.1630	12.8723	18.80	1.2051	13.0899	22.40	1.2485	13.3120
15.30	1.1642	12.8783	18.90	1.2063	13.0961	22.50	1.2497	13.3182
15.40	1.1653	12.8843	19.00	1.2075	13.1022	22.60	1.2509	13.3244
15.50	1.1665	12.8903	19.10	1.2086	13.1083	22.70	1.2522	13.3307
15.60	1.1677	12.8963	19.20	1.2098	13.1144	22.80	1.2534	13.3369
15.70	1.1688	12.9023	19.30	1.2110	13.1205	22.90	1.2546	13.3432
15.80	1.1700	12.9083	19.40	1.2122	13.1266	23.00	1.2559	13.3494
15.90	1.1711	12.9143	19.50	1.2134	13.1328	23.10	1.2571	13.3557
16.00	1.1723	12.9203	19.60	1.2146	13.1389	23.20	1.2583	13.3619
16.10	1.1734	12.9263	19.70	1.2158	13.1450	23.30	1.2596	13.3682
16.20	1.1746	12.9323	19.80	1.2170	13.1512	23.40	1.2608	13.3744
16.30	1.1757	12.9384	19.90	1.2182	13.1573	23.50	1.2620	13.3807
16.40	1.1769	12.9444	20.00	1.2194	13.1635	23.60	1.2633	13.3870
16.50	1.1781	12.9504	20.10	1.2206	13.1696	23.70	1.2645	13.3933
16.60	1.1792	12.9564	20.20	1.2218	13.1758	23.80	1.2658	13.3995
16.70	1.1804	12.9625	20.30	1.2230	13.1819	23.90	1.2670	13.4058
16.80	1.1816	12.9685	20.40	1.2242	13.1881	24.00	1.2682	13.4121
16.90	1.1827	12.9745	20.50	1.2254	13.1942	24.10	1.2695	13.4184
17.00	1.1839	12.9806	20.60	1.2266	13.2004	24.20	1.2707	13.4247
17.10	1.1851	12.9866	20.70	1.2278	13.2066	24.30	1.2720	13.4310
17.20	1.1862	12.9927	20.80	1.2290	13.2127	24.40	1.2732	13.4373
17.30	1.1874	12.9987	20.90	1.2302	13.2189	24.50	1.2745	13.4436
17.40	1.1886	13.0048	21.00	1.2314	13.2251	24.60	1.2757	13.4499
17.50	1.1897	13.0109	21.10	1.2327	13.2313	24.70	1.2770	13.4562
17.60	1.1909	13.0169	21.20	1.2339	13.2375	24.80	1.2782	13.4625
17.70	1.1921	13.0230	21.30	1.2351	13.2437	24.90	1.2795	13.4688
17.80	1.1933	13.0291	21.40	1.2363	13.2499	25.00	1.2807	13.4751
17.90	1.1944	13.0351	21.50	1.2375	13.2561	25.10	1.2820	13.4814
18.00	1.1956	13.0412	21.60	1.2387	13.2623	25.20	1.2832	13.4878
18.10	1.1968	13.0473	21.70	1.2399	13.2685	25.30	1.2845	13.4941
18.20	1.1980	13.0534	21.80	1.2412	13.2747	25.40	1.2858	13.5004
18.30	1.1992	13.0595	21.90	1.2424	13.2809	25.50	1.2870	13.5068

APPENDIX 3

TRUE APR FOR SECOND MORTGAGES

True APR for Second Mortgages

	TAX BRACKET				
Loan APR	**15.00%**	**28.00%**	**31.00%**	**36.00%**	**39.60%**
6.00%	5.10%	4.32%	4.14%	3.84%	3.62%
6.25%	5.31%	4.50%	4.31%	4.00%	3.78%
6.50%	5.53%	4.68%	4.49%	4.16%	3.93%
6.75%	5.74%	4.86%	4.66%	4.32%	4.08%
7.00%	5.95%	5.04%	4.83%	4.48%	4.23%
7.25%	6.16%	5.22%	5.00%	4.64%	4.38%
7.50%	6.38%	5.40%	5.18%	4.80%	4.53%
7.75%	6.59%	5.58%	5.35%	4.96%	4.68%
8.00%	6.80%	5.76%	5.52%	5.12%	4.83%
8.25%	7.01%	5.94%	5.69%	5.28%	4.98%
8.50%	7.23%	6.12%	5.87%	5.44%	5.13%
8.75%	7.44%	6.30%	6.04%	5.60%	5.29%
9.00%	7.65%	6.48%	6.21%	5.76%	5.44%
9.25%	7.86%	6.66%	6.38%	5.92%	5.59%
9.50%	8.08%	6.84%	6.56%	6.08%	5.74%
9.75%	8.29%	7.02%	6.73%	6.24%	5.89%
10.00%	8.50%	7.20%	6.90%	6.40%	6.04%
10.25%	8.71%	7.38%	7.07%	6.56%	6.19%
10.50%	8.93%	7.56%	7.25%	6.72%	6.34%
10.75%	9.14%	7.74%	7.42%	6.88%	6.49%
11.00%	9.35%	7.92%	7.59%	7.04%	6.64%
11.25%	9.56%	8.10%	7.76%	7.20%	6.80%
11.50%	9.78%	8.28%	7.94%	7.36%	6.95%
11.75%	9.99%	8.46%	8.11%	7.52%	7.10%
12.00%	10.20%	8.64%	8.28%	7.68%	7.25%
12.25%	10.41%	8.82%	8.45%	7.84%	7.40%
12.50%	10.63%	9.00%	8.63%	8.00%	7.55%
12.75%	10.84%	9.18%	8.80%	8.16%	7.70%
13.00%	11.05%	9.36%	8.97%	8.32%	7.85%
13.25%	11.26%	9.54%	9.14%	8.48%	8.00%
13.50%	11.48%	9.72%	9.32%	8.64%	8.15%
13.75%	11.69%	9.90%	9.49%	8.80%	8.31%
14.00%	11.90%	10.08%	9.66%	8.96%	8.46%
14.25%	12.11%	10.26%	9.83%	9.12%	8.61%
14.50%	12.33%	10.44%	10.01%	9.28%	8.76%
14.75%	12.54%	10.62%	10.18%	9.44%	8.91%

True APR for Second Mortgages

	TAX BRACKET				
Loan APR	15.00%	28.00%	31.00%	36.00%	39.60%
15.00%	12.75%	10.80%	10.35%	9.60%	9.06%
15.25%	12.96%	10.98%	10.52%	9.76%	9.21%
15.50%	13.18%	11.16%	10.70%	9.92%	9.36%
15.75%	13.39%	11.34%	10.87%	10.08%	9.51%
16.00%	13.60%	11.52%	11.04%	10.24%	9.66%
16.25%	13.81%	11.70%	11.21%	10.40%	9.82%
16.50%	14.03%	11.88%	11.39%	10.56%	9.97%
16.75%	14.24%	12.06%	11.56%	10.72%	10.12%
17.00%	14.45%	12.24%	11.73%	10.88%	10.27%
17.25%	14.66%	12.42%	11.90%	11.04%	10.42%
17.50%	14.88%	12.60%	12.08%	11.20%	10.57%
17.75%	15.09%	12.78%	12.25%	11.36%	10.72%
18.00%	15.30%	12.96%	12.42%	11.52%	10.87%
18.25%	15.51%	13.14%	12.59%	11.68%	11.02%
18.50%	15.73%	13.32%	12.77%	11.84%	11.17%
18.75%	15.94%	13.50%	12.94%	12.00%	11.33%
19.00%	16.15%	13.68%	13.11%	12.16%	11.48%
19.25%	16.36%	13.86%	13.28%	12.32%	11.63%
19.50%	16.58%	14.04%	13.46%	12.48%	11.78%
19.75%	16.79%	14.22%	13.63%	12.64%	11.93%
20.00%	17.00%	14.40%	13.80%	12.80%	12.08%
20.25%	17.21%	14.58%	13.97%	12.96%	12.23%
20.50%	17.43%	14.76%	14.15%	13.12%	12.38%
20.75%	17.64%	14.94%	14.32%	13.28%	12.53%
21.00%	17.85%	15.12%	14.49%	13.44%	12.68%
21.25%	18.06%	15.30%	14.66%	13.60%	12.84%
21.50%	18.28%	15.48%	14.84%	13.76%	12.99%
21.75%	18.49%	15.66%	15.01%	13.92%	13.14%
22.00%	18.70%	15.84%	15.18%	14.08%	13.29%
22.25%	18.91%	16.02%	15.35%	14.24%	13.44%
22.50%	19.13%	16.20%	15.53%	14.40%	13.59%
22.75%	19.34%	16.38%	15.70%	14.56%	13.74%
23.00%	19.55%	16.56%	15.87%	14.72%	13.89%
23.25%	19.76%	16.74%	16.04%	14.88%	14.04%
23.50%	19.98%	16.92%	16.22%	15.04%	14.19%
23.75%	20.19%	17.10%	16.39%	15.20%	14.35%

INDEX

A

Account Agreement.................................. 22
Account information required................... 55
Annual Fee 24, 84, 86, 95, 103
Annual Percentage Rate 33, 85
   Calculating... 42
APR ....*See* Annual Percentage Rate
APR_M.. 58
Auto loan... 46
Auto rebates 107
Available Credit...........................57, 61, 70
Average Daily Balance............................ 33

B

Bad Advice...109
Balance & Payment Factors 88, 132
Balance Factor... 88
Balance transfers 83, 95, 103, 107, 108
Bank policies 22
Bankcard Holders of America 78
Bankruptcy.. 81
Bill-Pay Day.............................97, 102, 104
Bills...96, 101
Bills-Unpaid File.................. 20, 21, 97, 102
Budgeting 72

C

Calculating Savings 75
Calculating the unpaid balance................ 43
Canceled Checks......................................101
Cash Advances 73, 83, 84, 86, 103
   Fees and policies 24
Cash back refunds 103
Cash-back refunds 95
Checking Account.................................... 15
   Balancing... 98
Checking Account Balancing Worksheet .. 98
Closed-end..................... *See* Types of Credit
Clutter...97, 104
Comparing Cards & Loans 86
Computers... 13
Credit card debt 11
Credit Card Graveyard..............21, 104, 105
Credit Card InfoSheet 22, 55, 78, 86, 102

Credit cards...12
   Choosing...83
   Secured...15
Credit history 11, 12, 15, 105
Credit limit..................................... 95, 103
Credit management 10
Credit Offer InfoSheet 22, 78, 102, 103
Credit Offers 21, 24, 103
Credit repair companies 107
Credit report.............................. 104, 108
Credit Solutions.......................................72
Cross-over point 90

D

Debt..58, 61
Debt Management 18, 79, 109
Denied credit 108
Discipline...13
Disclaimer...7
Divisor...24
Dollar-Weighted Average Interest Rate58, 61

E

Emergency fund.......................................113
Employers 12
Equifax ....*See* Credit report
Equity 78
Example
   5.1 (Calculating Interest Charges) 33
   5.2 (Calculating APR)............................34
   5.3 (Calculating the RATIO)................36
   5.4 (Using tables to find RATIO) 38
   5.5 (Using tables for Time Remaining) ..38
   5.6 (Using tables for APR) 39
   5.7 (Calculating the Monthly Payment)..40
   5.8 (Calculating the Time Remaining) ...41
   5.9 (Finding the APR) 42
   5.10 (Finding the Principal)...................43
   5.11 (Finding the Unpaid Balance) 45
   5.12 (Auto Loan Principal)....................46
   5.13 (Payment Plan or Credit Card).......47
   6.1 (Model Example) 54
   8.1 (Net Income).................................66

9.1 (Calculating Savings) 75
10.1 (Finding cash advance fees) 85
10.2 (Finding cash advance fees) 85
10.3 (Balance & Payment Factors) 88
10.4 (Credit card comparison) 87
10.5 (Credit card comparison) 90
10.6 (Credit card comparison) 92
10.7 (Credit card comparison) 94
13.1 (Home equity loan vs. Credit card)111
13.2 (True APR for Second Mortgages)113
13.3 (Emergency Fund) 114
Example Worksheets
    Credit Card InfoSheet.......................... 26
    Credit Offer InfoSheets....................... 27
    Loan Calculation Worksheet............... 62
    Payment Schedule Worksheet 68
Expenses 67

F

Fees.. 83
    Cash Advance fees and Policies 24
Figure
    5.1 (Cash Flow Diagram) 35
    5.2 (Time-Remaining Table)................ 37
    7.1 (Loan Calc. Worksheet - example 6.1)62
    8.1 (Payment Schedule for example 6.1) 68
    9.1 (Transferring balances)................... 73
    9.2 (New Loan Calculation Worksheet for
        example 6.1) 74
    9.5 (New Payment Schedule for example
        6.1)... 77
    11.1 (Bill-Pay Calendar)...................... 97
    11.2 (Sorting the Bills-Unpaid File) 98
    13.1 (True APR for Home Equity).......112
Files 19, 20, 106
Financial calculators 13
Financial plans.................................86, 87
Fixed interest rate 94, 103
Float...104
Frequent flyer miles 107
Future value 44, 86, 88

G

Getting Credit...................................... 15
Goals... 72

H

Habits..103
Happiness... 18

Home equity loans 111

I

Incentives 94
Income 65
Int Rate 61
Interest...35, 36
Interest payments..................................72
Interest rate 32, 33, 85, 86, 95
    Finding lower rates................. 73, 78, 106
Introduction..8
Introductory rates 103

L

Landlords..12
Laws..11
Left over weekly...................................70
Liability 108
Loan Calculation Worksheet. 61, 74, 98, 102
Loans...32
Lost or stolen.......................................108

M

MAC..99
Mail..96, 103
    Sorting...21
Management...11
Math 108
Math and Money 31
Max 61
Maximum Lending Time....................23, 24
Maximum Limit.....................................56
Minimum Monthly Payment Policy 95
Minimum Payment 81, 101
Minimum Payment Policy...................24, 81
Minimum Weekly 70
Model...18, 54, 61
    Accuracy of...79
    Elements...56
    Example 6.1..54
Monthly Payment 61, 66, 86, 103
    Calculating 39
Mortgage..66
    Second Mortgages...............................113

N

Negative Amortization..............................81
Nilson Report 11

O

Open-end........................ *See* Types of Credit
Open-end equity............. *See* Types of Credit
Organization... 19
Outstanding balance................. *See* Principal
Overdraft protection................................105

P

Payment Factor....................................... 88
Payment Schedule... 65, 70, 96, 98, 101, 102
Payments.................. 32, 34, 35, 36, 58, 104
   Skipping..106
Payoff penalties 107
Payoff Time....................................60, 61
Periodic payments..............................34, 66
Perks ....*See* Incentives
Phone Charges.. 67
Planning 18
Pre-Approved credit offers 103
Press One Publishing 2, 7
Principal........................ 32, 35, 36, 61, 86
   Calculating.. 43
Principal x Int Rate................................. 61
Problems 48

R

RATIO..36, 61
Real-Life Examples 46
Record keeping.......................................106
Relationships 35
Rent 66
Road map 12

S

Savings............110   *See* Calculating Savings
Savings account..................................... 15
Schedule A 111
Second Mortgages 78, 113
Secured credit card 15
Secured Loans 78
Secured, closed-end........ *See* Types of Credit
Secured, open-end.......... *See* Types of Credit
Shopping list.. 19
Shorter terms 106

T

Simplification...18
Solutions to problems 50
Sorting Mail 21
Spending categories 67

T

Tax bracket 111
Terms...107, 109
Time 32, 34, 35, 36
Time Remaining (Calculating) 41
Time-Remaining Tables........ 23, 25, 36, 116
Tips 103
Trans Union ....*See* Credit report
Transaction Register................................99
True APR for Second Mortgages 135
TRW...............................*See* Credit report
Types of Credit
   Open-end equity....................................15
   Secured, closed-end...............................14
   Secured, open-end.................................15
   Unsecured, closed-end...........................15
   Unsecured, open-end.............................14

U

Unpaid balance.............................23, 43, 86
Unsecured, closed-end ....*See* Types of Credit
Unsecured, open-end.......*See* Types of Credit

W

Warning 7
Warning Signs...16
Work area 97
Worksheet Usage Summary
   Credit Card InfoSheet 23
   Credit Offer InfoSheet..........................23
   Loan Calculation Worksheet 61
   Payment Schedule Worksheet................69
Worksheets..................... 9, 12, 96, 102, 108
Worksheets (blank)
   Checking Account Balancing Worksheet100
   Credit Card InfoSheet 29
   Credit Offer InfoSheet..........................30
   Loan Calculation Worksheet 64
   Payment Schedule 71

ORDER FORM

☎ **TELEPHONE ORDERS:** (609) 660-0682

✹ **FAX ORDERS:** (609) 660-1412

🖥 **E-MAIL ORDERS:** PressOne@CyberComm.Net

✉ **MAIL ORDER:** Press One Publishing, PO Box 563, Barnegat, NJ 08005-0563

CREDIT CARD AND DEBT MANAGEMENT (ISBN 0-9648401-9-7): $19.95

SALES TAX: New Jersey residents please add 6%.

PRIORITY MAIL SHIPPING: $4.00 for the first book and $1.25 for each additional book.

Name: _____

Address: _____

City: _____ State: _____ Zip: _____

Telephone: (____) _____

Please send me _____ copy(ies) at $19.95 each = $ _____

Plus tax (6% for NJ residents) = + $ _____

Plus shipping ($4 for first book $1.25 for each additional) = + $ _____

TOTAL = $ _____

PAYMENT: ☐ Check ☐ Cash ☐ Money Order
☐ MasterCard ☐ VISA ☐ AmEx

Credit Card #: _____

Expiration date: _____

Signature: _____

Order Today!

ORDER FORM

☎ **TELEPHONE ORDERS:** (609) 660-0682

✳ **FAX ORDERS:** (609) 660-1412

🖳 **E-MAIL ORDERS:** PressOne@CyberComm.Net

✉ **MAIL ORDER:** Press One Publishing, PO Box 563, Barnegat, NJ 08005-0563

CREDIT CARD AND DEBT MANAGEMENT (ISBN 0-9648401-9-7): $19.95

SALES TAX: New Jersey residents please add 6%.

PRIORITY MAIL SHIPPING: $4.00 for the first book and $1.25 for each additional book.

Name: _____

Address: _____

City: _____ State: _____ Zip: _____

Telephone: (____) _____

Please send me _____ copy(ies) at $19.95 each = $ _____

Plus tax (6% for NJ residents) = + $ _____

Plus shipping ($4 for first book $1.25 for each additional) = + $ _____

TOTAL = $ _____

PAYMENT: ☐ Check ☐ Cash ☐ Money Order
☐ MasterCard ☐ VISA ☐ AmEx

Credit Card #: _____

Expiration date: _____

Signature: _____

Order Today!